Haunted Places of Middlesex

Mike Hall

COUNTRYSIDE BOOKS
NEWBURY, BERKSHIRE

First Published 2004

COUNTRYSIDE BOOKS
3 Catherine Road
Newbury, Berkshire

To view our complete range of books,
please visit us at
www..countrysidebooks.co.uk

ISBN 1 85306 857 8

This book is dedicated to the memory of the Rotary Club of
Sunbury-on-Thames (1945–2003), now sadly defunct.
Perhaps the phantoms of its erstwhile members – including me –
may be seen once more in the Ship Hotel at Shepperton
or one of our earlier haunts !

Cover picture from an original
painting by Anthony Wallis

Designed by Peter Davies, Nautilus Design
Typeset by Mac Style Ltd, Scarborough, N. Yorkshire
Produced through MRM Associates Ltd., Reading
Printed by Cromwell Press, Trowbridge

Contents

• Introduction •

Recently a teenage girl at the school in Sunbury where I teach told me a strange story. She swears that it is true. 'It was when I was little,' she said. 'Something woke me in the middle of the night. I got out of bed and looked out of the window. Outside I saw clearly the figure of my uncle – who had died unexpectedly in Scotland just a few days before.'

Perhaps she had just had a dream about him – not unlikely in the circumstances – but to this day she is convinced that she saw a ghost!

In 2001 psychologist Dr Richard Wiseman of the University of Hertfordshire conducted an investigation into the legendary Haunted Gallery at Hampton Court Palace. Using 450 volunteers he discovered that at least half of them reported one or more unusual experiences. Often it was a drop in temperature or a strong sense of the presence of something – or someone. Many doubtless would attribute these to some supernatural agency but, sadly for these romantics, the results of Dr Wiseman's thermal imaging experiments led him to conclude that most were due to columns of cold air caused by concealed doors and the like.

Many scientific studies have attempted to debunk the very notion of ghosts. Dr Wiseman himself wrote in the *New Scientist* magazine that such experiences could be explained by a combination of fear and the effects of electromagnetic fields, temperature changes and geological conditions.

Yet still the legends persist and not all academics are so sure that they can be dismissed so lightly. Professor Ian Stevenson, a senior clinical psychiatrist at the University of Virginia, wrote in 1944, after forty years studying reports of ghosts in Britain and the United States, that they could not be disregarded as merely the rantings of the insane or the work of hoaxers – 'evidence of these kinds of experiences are too frequent to be dismissed, he said.

Hampton Court Palace is alleged to be one of the most haunted buildings in Britain, hardly surprising in view of its turbulent and sometimes bloody history but, according to the highly-respected Ghost Society, a phantom is more likely to be reported in an ordinary location than in a stately home or dungeon.

My research into haunted places of Middlesex would tend to support this. One of the most famous paranormal cases in modern times – 'The Enfield Poltergeist' – happened in an ordinary council house. Where my stories concern people's homes, please respect the privacy of the present occupants. These places, although often easily identifiable, are in no sense open to the public. The owners of the many haunted pubs, on the other hand, would I'm sure be delighted to discuss their stories over a few pints.

The great and the good are here as well – Erasmus at Shepperton, Alexander Pope at Twickenham and even the scandalous Duchess of Cleveland at Chiswick. Osterley, Kensington Palace and Bruce Castle, as well as Hampton Court, all have their ghost stories.

I have travelled all over the former county of Middlesex in search of the supernatural. Some of the tales are tragic, some frankly bizarre, like the phantom frozen chicken that lurks in Pond Square at Highgate. Purists might note that my definition of Middlesex has been somewhat elastic. The familiar outline of the old county shown on the map dates from the Local Government Act of 1883 but I strayed across this boundary to include tales from places like Chiswick, Kensington, Islington and Hackney which were villages within the historic county before being swamped by the spread of London. In one case I even followed the phantoms through the underground passage that leads from Sutton House at Hackney, under the River Lea, and emerges in St Mary's churchyard in my childhood home parish of Leyton in what was once Essex – but that is as far as my travels led me.

I am grateful to the many people who gave me stories for this book and also to the many researchers whose works I consulted. The latter are listed in the bibliography and are well worth searching for.

Mike Hall

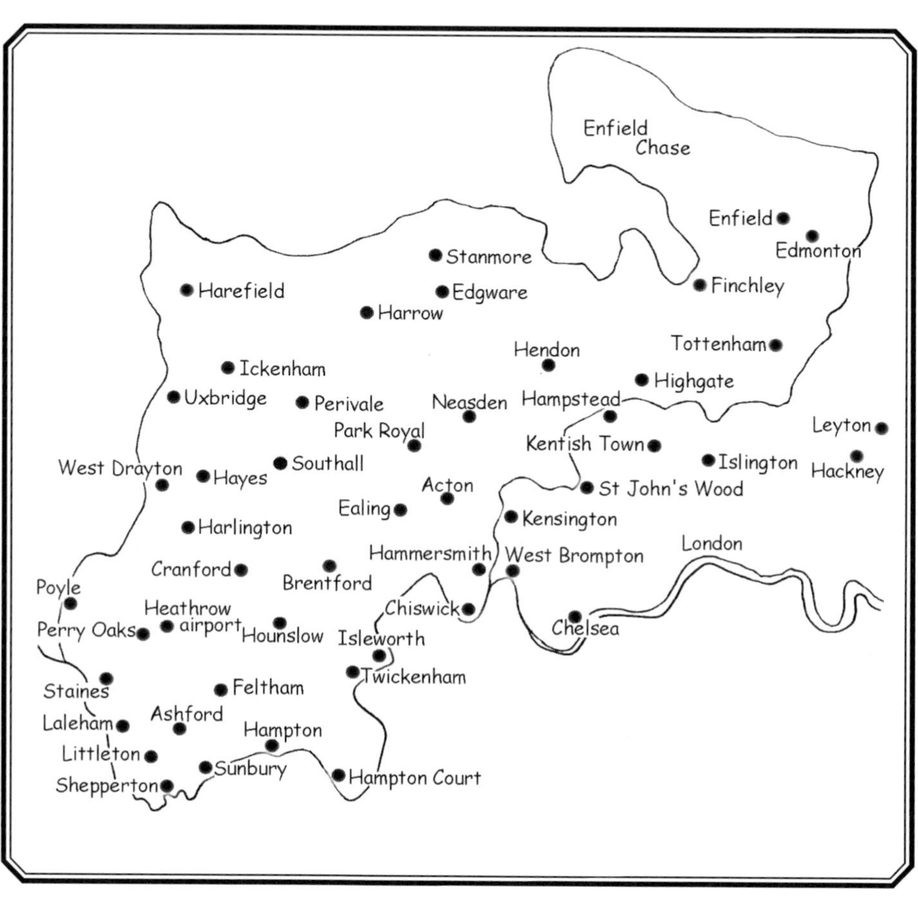
Enfield
Chase
Enfield
Edmonton
Stanmore
Harefield
Edgware
Finchley
Harrow
Hendon
Tottenham
Ickenham
Highgate
Uxbridge
Perivale
Neasden
Hampstead
Park Royal
Leyton
Kentish Town
Islington
Hackney
West Drayton
Southall
Hayes
Acton
St John's Wood
Ealing
Kensington
Harlington
Hammersmith
West Brompton
London
Cranford
Brentford
Poyle
Heathrow
airport
Chiswick
Perry Oaks
Hounslow
Isleworth
Chelsea
Twickenham
Staines
Feltham
Laleham
Ashford
Hampton
Littleton
Sunbury
Shepperton
Hampton Court

Sweet William's Ghost

(a verse from a traditional ballad sung by Kate Rushby on her CD 'Underneath the Stars', Pure Records, 2003)

No more the ghost to Margaret came
With many a grievous groan.
He's vanished out into the mist,
And left her there alone.
Oh stay, my only true love, stay.
My heart you do divide.
Pale grew her cheeks, she closed her eyes,
Stretched out her limbs and cried.

•Blood Staines•

The Black Boy of Duncroft

Duncroft House, Staines.

Away from the bustle of Staines High Street with its modern shopping centres, Church Street leads to a quieter part of town where there are still some gracious houses. One of these is Duncroft House, which lies between Moor Lane and Wraysbury Road, now converted into luxury flats and concealing a chequered past. It has been variously a Dr Barnado's home, an approved school and between 1847 and 1892 it was owned by the Ashby family who were noted Quakers and benefactors to the town.

The Duncroft estate can be traced back to the thirteenth century. There are various legends rather optimistically linking the place to the granting of the Magna Carta in 1215. It has been claimed that King John slept at Duncroft the night before putting his signature to the historic document but sadly it is more likely that he stayed at Windsor Castle. In any event, he would not recognise any of the present building which dates from no earlier than 1600.

Like so many other old houses, Duncroft is reputed to have an underground passage and was said to be haunted by a black boy who, at some time in the past, was murdered by a cook. The poor lad is supposed to have fallen, or more likely been pushed, into a vat of boiling oil. The boy, apart from the usual ghostly repertoire of knocking on walls and opening doors, is claimed to have caused forty dogs, who were running loose in the house, to suddenly stand still, their hair rising in fright. This, of course, begs the question of why so many dogs were running wild in the building in the first place! Come to that – why the vat of boiling oil?

It is said that a local priest was called in to rid the house of this malevolent spirit. The reverend gentleman suggested that it would help if the lad had somewhere else to go and an insignificant alley off the High Street was renamed Black Boy Lane. This seemed to do the trick and, even though the alley disappeared in the nineteenth-century redevelopment of the area, Duncroft no longer suffers his attentions.

Not far from Staines, on the edge of the parish of Stanwell, lay Poyle Manor. Poyle these days is an industrial estate, part of Slough and in South Buckinghamshire, but in Tudor times it was a quiet and attractive rural part of Middlesex. In 1587 Queen Elizabeth I gave the manor to Nicholas Hilliard, her celebrated portrait painter and miniaturist who designed her Great Seals.

The manor house, which sadly was destroyed by fire in the 1930s, was believed to have been haunted by The Grey Lady, the wronged wife of a Cavalier who owned it around the time of the Civil War. The story goes that one day this poor lady saw her husband dallying with 'a proper hussy' in a boat on the River Colne that flowed through the grounds. Clearly what was going on was most improper and she was devastated by what she saw.

When her husband returned to the house his wife was nowhere to be seen. Alarmed, and doubtless feeling somewhat guilty, he had his servants search the estate. It was not long before her body was found drowned in the river.

From then on her ghost reappeared from time to time, dressed in her habitual sombre grey, and said to be searching for her feckless husband.

The Curse of Laleham Church

Laleham, by the River Thames in west Middlesex, is nowadays more or less part of Staines but in 1933, when the King family moved into the village, it was still largely a rural community. They moved in on Good

Laleham church interior in 1908, two years before the ill-fated alterations. (Laleham Heritage Centre)

Friday. There were two children, Peter, aged ten months, and Kathleen, who was nearly two. They came from Feltham, just a few miles away but far enough for them to be considered outsiders. Mr King was a coal delivery man and through his work discovered that number 2 Plumtree Cottages, a mid-terrace property now prosaically known as 67 Ashford Road, was about to become vacant. At number 1 lived two maiden sisters, Miss Harriet and Miss May Perry. Mrs Mason and her daughter Lucy lived at number 3.

Number 2 had been used by the Perry family to house their invalid brother. He had been severely injured while working on alterations to the ancient village church, being made at the instigation of the Lucan family who were Lords of the Manor in 1910. He had fallen from scaffolding and was to remain bedridden for the rest of his life – the victim, it would appear, of an ancient curse.

According to Mrs Mason at 3 Plumtree Cottages, some eminent worthy long ago (she did not know who) had put a curse on anyone altering the church in any way. No-one took much notice at the time, such threats are commonplace. Most church congregations will know of some long-serving churchwarden or similar who has seen many changes in the church in their lifetime – and resisted every one! 'No good will come of it, mark my words, Vicar!'

Yet in 1910 after a picture of St Peter walking on the water was trimmed, ancient pews removed (one to end up in the Miss Perrys' garden) and an old altar moved against a wall, strange things began to happen – culminating in the tragic accident that befell Bob Perry.

The King family soon became conscious of strange things happening in their cottage. Doors would mysteriously open and footsteps were often heard upstairs when there was nobody there. Things seemed to be particularly bad on Sunday mornings. There was no such thing as central heating in those days so it could not have been the noise of the water pipes.

It was only then that they learned that after his accident Bob's friends in the old Laleham Band had been in the habit of going upstairs to play for him on Sunday mornings after church. 'For an hour or so there would always be a commotion,' Peter King recalled in a book of Laleham memories published in 1989, 'but we learned to live with it.'

Albert Attfield, the last member of the old Laleham village band, passed away in 1948. 'After that,' Peter wrote, 'our cottage became silent and still. The noises in the bedroom ceased, doors remained closed and a tranquility – and yet an emptiness – remained until, sadly, both my parents departed from 67 Ashford Road in late 1986.'

In the early twentieth century villagers in Laleham, like simple country folk everywhere, were suspicious of banks and preferred to keep their spare cash (if they had any) at home. One man living with his daughter in School Cottages, Laleham, had quite a tidy sum hidden away under the floorboards. He became ill, so ill that he was thought to be dying. His daughter, who knew about her father's secret store of money, obviously felt that a timely donation to the Almighty might ease his path into Heaven. She removed the cash from its hiding place and gave it all to the Church.

As things turned out, the old man did not die at that time and, when he heard what his daughter had done, he was not best pleased. He died subsequently but was said to return to the cottages from time to time, to look for his money. This was apparently so disturbing that in the early 1970s the then vicar of Laleham carried out an exorcism there.

Of course, the Lucan family, Lords of the Manor, is still remembered in Laleham. They too perhaps also have their curse – from the ill-fated military commander in the Charge of the Light Brigade – to 'Lucky', the Lord Lucan whose disappearance in 1974 has been a cause of speculation ever since.

THE MATRIARCH AND THE MIDNIGHT CHILDREN

There are a number of large eighteenth-century houses in Laleham. An elderly couple who lived in one of them for many years became accustomed to the presence of one of their predecessors in the house, a lady who I'll call 'The Matriarch'. They became quite unconcerned by these appearances and spoke to neighbours about them in a very matter-of-fact way.

The two old people eventually died and the house was sold. The new owners, not unreasonably, wanted to modernise the place, including putting in a new kitchen and bathroom. They got a team of young Scots to do the work and, as they had not yet moved in, allowed the lads to live there while it was being done. All seemed to be going well although neighbours were a little surprised to see the lights left on all night – surely the men were not working twenty-four hours a day?

One day the lady who, with her husband, had bought the property came to see how the work was progressing. Afterwards, somewhat anxiously, she asked a neighbour whether he knew anything about the history of the house. In particular, she wanted to know whether he had heard of any ghosts there.

It appeared that the workmen had been seriously alarmed by what they had experienced late at night. In the first incident one of them had needed to visit the bathroom during the night. On his way he encountered the figure of a small boy sitting on the stairs. He was so unnerved by this unexpected apparition that from then on anyone needing to make similar nocturnal journeys made sure that one of the others accompanied them!

Some time afterwards a new concrete floor was laid down and left overnight to dry. The next morning the workmen discovered a child's footprint together with what seemed to be a set of cat's pawprints. These went right across the floor and disappeared into the wall, as if continuing beyond it.

Despite these happenings the new owners moved in and lived in the house quite happily for several years. However, in the fortnight before they moved out, their sleep was disturbed by what sounded like young children's voices, apparently coming from rooms at the top of the house.

It all seems very odd, the various disturbances taking place at the times when the property was changing hands. 'The Matriarch' seemed to have been replaced by images of children. It is known that during the nineteenth century several of the old houses in Laleham were occupied by private schools, some of them rather short-lived. Perhaps there had been a school in this particular house.

Erasmus at Shepperton

The architectural historian Sir Nikolaus Pevsner, writing in 1951, described Church Square at Shepperton as 'one of the most perfect village pictures Middlesex has to offer'. It is still picturesque today, especially if you manage to see it when it is not cluttered with cars!

Standing back from the square, to the left of the church, is the Rectory. What Pevsner describes as 'an exquisite front of c.1700' conceals an interior that is two centuries older. It also, if local legend is to be believed, conceals the ghost of the Dutch scholar from the time of the Renaissance, Erasmus of Rotterdam.

Quite why this eminent figure should haunt the Rectory is not clear. He is known to have been a friend of the Reverend William Grocyn who held the living of Shepperton from 1504 to 1513. Erasmus is believed to have visited Grocyn at Shepperton and would have stood under the same moulded beams that grace the spacious hall to this day.

Shepperton Rectory.

A twentieth-century successor to William Grocyn was Reverend Henry McLeod, who was rector for ten years from 1927. It is said that one of his children, a young girl, was ill in bed upstairs and saw a figure dressed in sixteenth-century clothes standing in the bedroom. This must have alarmed her considerably and she was even more disconcerted later when she visited Hampton Court and recognised the same figure in Holbein's portrait of Erasmus on display there.

This indentification may be mistaken. Angela Ball, whose husband Peter was rector in the 1970s, believed that the child may indeed have seen someone in Tudor clothes and been misled into thinking that the similarly-dressed man in the portrait was the person she saw.

One day in Mr McLeod's time a prospective curate arrived at the Rectory. The rector was out and one of his sisters asked him to take a seat in the hall to await his return. While he was waiting he heard someone come down the stairs but when he looked round (or up from his newspaper) there was no-one there. When told of this, Miss McLeod said that she often heard footsteps on the stairs. Peter Ball, who later became a Canon of St Paul's Cathedral, met the young man in question there decades later and it is he who provided this story.

The staircase in the fifteenth and sixteenth century descended the opposite way to the present one. Angela Ball recalled how one evening she was alone in the Rectory while the rest of the family were at the church for Evensong. Standing at the bottom of the stairs reading a letter, she heard the heavy pages of a large book being turned, as if someone was standing at an ancient reading desk. The noise came from her son Michael's room. At first she thought he must be in there but then realised that he wasn't.

Reverend Chris Swift, the present incumbent, told me that he had never seen the apparition. Neither had his dog – and animals have often been shown to be particularly sensitive to supernatural phenomena. However his daughter had apparently experienced something odd, as had some other residents in recent years.

Next door to the Rectory is the Anchor Hotel much frequented in its heyday by stars from the Shepperton Film Studios, including Rex Harrison and Kay

The Anchor Hotel, Shepperton.

Kendall. Legend has it – and this particular legend is clearly good for business – that in the eighteenth century the hotel was a regular haunt of Dick Turpin, fresh from his exploits on Hounslow Heath. A pistol allegedly found in the rafters bore the chilling inscription 'Dick's Friend'! In the years before the Second World War the inn was actually owned by a family named Turpin but, sadly, they were not related to the infamous highwayman.

There are several ghostly tales associated with the Anchor and in the summer of 2003 local journalist Patsy Duffy visited the inn in the company of Neil Dudman, founder of Paranormal Investigations (based in Hampshire) and mediums Marion Goodfellow and Paul Hanrahan. Afterwards Patsy reported that 'Marion detected a preacher, possibly from the pilgrim era, outside the hotel. She said he was a regular visitor and detected the name Samuel. As he followed us in Marion started to draw what she felt about him. The picture bore a likeness to Victorian statesman Benjamin Disraeli.'

Marion had not known in advance where she was being taken so it is curious that the panelling in the functions room is traditionally said to have come from Disraeli's home at Hughenden in Buckinghamshire. However the National Trust, who own that property, have no record of panelling being removed from Hughenden. It is now thought that the panelling may have come from Disraeli's father's house at nearby Bradenham.

'As we walked down the corridor to the Disraeli Room,' Patsy wrote, 'there was a distinct change in temperature.' Pictures taken there have shown a series of orbs of light shooting along the corridor. These orbs are said to indicate a spirit presence or energy. 'Neil thought he saw a figure about four to five feet tall in the restaurant area. Marion also felt the presence of a girl aged about seven or eight.' The presence of this little girl, apparently, ties in with reported sightings by hotel staff. Marion was also aware of 'a woman who may have died of fever in the Oliver Room, once the mistress of the house, rather than the owner'.

Patsy, it has to be said, felt none of this – 'I hoped beyond hope I would witness my first sighting,' she said. 'Alas, it was not meant to be.' But, even if there are ghosts at the Anchor, guests have no need to worry. The hotel's owner, Douglas Gordon, commented 'So long as they are friendly ghosts, we don't really mind.'

Across Church Road from the hotel, Anchor Cottage, which dates back three hundred years, has the ghost of a little girl which has been seen to walk through a wall of this much-altered property. Sally Dick, who lived there for many years, told me, 'Sometimes you can hear her footsteps upstairs. She's surprisingly heavy footed but she doesn't worry or scare me.' Could she be the same child that has been seen in the hotel?

THE PHANTOM PLANE CRASH

First World War flying veteran Captain W.J. Gibson was only too familiar with the sound of an aircraft in difficulties. Late one evening in the winter of 1932 he was sitting in the lounge of his bungalow in Ferry Lane, Shepperton, when the dread sound was heard overhead.

Ferry Lane, Shepperton. The phantom plane was heard from the houses beyond the wall on the right.

'That plane's in trouble,' he said to his wife in alarm. As he finished speaking there was the sickening sound of the crash and the crumpling of the stricken machine. The Gibsons rushed out into the darkness fearing the worst – but there was no plane, no wreckage, no bodies to recover. A neighbour, Mrs Harding, had also heard the ominous sounds and had got up out of bed to rush to help – but there was no need. Together the Gibsons and Mrs Harding searched the damp riverside meadows but they found nothing.

But just three years before an aircraft *had* crashed in those self-same meadows. In the winter of 1929 a Vickers Vanguard had broken up at 4,000 feet and crashed in a field only a few hundred yards away from the Gibsons' bungalow. The pilot, Captain E.R. Scholefield and his mechanic, F.W. Cherrett, were killed instantly.

'I was on a boat on the Thames when Captain Scholefield's plane crashed.' Mrs Harding recalled. 'One wing came off the aircraft and crashed into the water near me. I can remember the sound very clearly and what I heard tonight was exactly the same.' The Gibsons too were certain of what they had heard.

Next morning they made enquiries among their neighbours. Others too had heard the sounds of an approaching plane, engine stuttering and then a crash. Some claimed actually to have seen it 'surrounded by a leadenish blue light'. Mrs Turpin, landlady of the Anchor Hotel in Church Square, saw what she described as a 'white and misty shape' and heard its eerie droning . Just before the phantom plane dived towards the ground, some claimed, dogs nearby had started howling dismally. And yet there was nothing to be found.

The same thing happened on six or seven nights, always around midnight. Mrs Harding got quite philosophical about the nightly intrusion. 'In the end I just said to myself – oh, there's the phantom plane again – and went back to sleep,' but other Shepperton residents became alarmed. It was suggested that the rector should hold a service of exorcism to lay the ghost to rest. But then the plane's nightly visits suddenly ceased and, as far as I know, being a Shepperton resident myself, the phantom plane was never heard or seen again.

STRANGE THINGS IN SUNBURY

'The night was very dark. A damp mist rose from the river and the marshy ground about and spread itself over the dreary fields. It was piercing cold too, all was gloomy and black. Not a word was spoken for the driver had grown sleepy and Sikes was in no mood to lead him in conversation. Oliver sat huddled together in a corner of the cart, bewildered with alarm and apprehension and figuring strange objects in the gaunt trees whose branches waved grimly to and fro, as if in some fantastic joy at the desolation of the scene.

'As they passed Sunbury Church, the clock struck seven. There was a light in the ferry house opposite which streamed across the road and threw into more sombre shadow a dark yew tree with graves beneath it. There was a dull

Fordbridge (formerly Watersplash) Road, Sunbury on Thames.

sound of water not far off and the leaves of the old tree stirred gently in the night wind. It seemed like quiet music for the repose of the dead.'

Charles Dickens was a frequent visitor to the village of Sunbury-on-Thames. This passage from *Oliver Twist* chillingly evokes the sinister atmosphere on the riverside on a murky winter's evening. *Oliver Twist* is not a ghost story but there are some strange tales associated with Sunbury.

One of the most curious concerns a phantom hearse. On a dark evening in November 1915, a Colonel Leland was being driven by his chauffeur Webber along Watersplash Road – now known as Fordbridge Road. Leaving the Colonel's house, they had gone two or three hundred yards when they saw a moving light on their left. Thinking it was a horse-drawn vehicle waiting to turn into Watersplash Road, the Colonel ordered Webber to slow down and give way to it. He did so and the mysterious vehicle, which was very indistinct, drew in and turned the way that Leland and Webber were travelling.

Intrigued, Colonel Leland told Webber to go up close behind it but not to pass. He did so and they followed closely for about two hundred yards. Leland could now plainly see the back of the vehicle. It was black and appeared to be a hearse. It was moving at a trot.

'The queer part was, I could see no driver,' the Colonel recalled later. The two panels at the back and the keyhole for locking the doors showed up most distinctly under the rays of our lamps.' As they approached a bend in the narrow road Leland and Webber hung back but once round the bend they accelerated to catch up – the road ahead was empty!

'Lord, Sir. What was that?' the astonished chauffeur cried. They went past the Flower Pot Inn, and drove on into the village but no trace of the driverless hearse could be found. Both the Colonel and his chauffeur were adamant about what they had seen and also that there had been no side road down which the hearse could have turned while after it had gone round the corner.

The former Castle Inn (now the Blue Dragon restaurant), Sunbury on Thames.

At the other end of Thames Street in Sunbury is the former Castle Inn, now a Chinese restaurant. It is an early seventeenth century building with a fine mansard roof. During the nineteenth century this establishment advertised 'well-aired beds, good stabling, accommodation for small or large parties, breakfast supplied on the shortest notice.' What the proprietors did not advertise however, was that there was a room alleged to be haunted. A spiral staircase gives access to the 'soldiers' room', a small uncomfortable room under the eaves which, by law at that time, every inn had to provide to accommodate the military in time of need. Perhaps they were anxious not to scare off nervous visitors.

I wonder whether the present owners are aware of the building's sinister history. Maybe it needs a touch of 'feng shui' to exorcise the ghost!

Hawke House in Green Street was built in 1703 and is named after Admiral Lord Hawke (1705–1781) who lived there for the last ten years of his life. He is famed in naval history as the victor of decisive sea battles against the French off Finisterre in 1747 and Quiberon Bay in 1759. Hawke House was the haven he retired to in his declining years. He must have loved it because several later owners and tenants of the property reported seeing his ghost in the house. The old seadog must have been saddened to see the historic features of the interior disappear when the building – admittedly already in poor repair after many years of neglect – was gutted and converted into offices during the 1970s. Perhaps he was tempted to decamp across the road to the Victorian pub that had been renamed in his honour about ten years before.

Sunbury Fire Station on the Staines Road West dual carriageway is a modern utilitarian building that might seem unlikely to harbour a ghost. Yet the station's Watch Commander, Roy Nottrodt told the local paper in March 2004 of a 'mysterious presence' there. It seems that he was asleep at the station one night when his bed and mattress started shaking violently. None of his colleagues believed his story the next morning and they pulled his leg mercilessly about the incident – but apparently the station cook is reluctant to go into certain areas of the building and someone once saw a face framed in the pole-hole window.

•Hampton Court Hauntings•

Three Queens and a Cardinal

Blue-blooded phantoms abound at Hampton Court Palace as one might expect in a place with so much history attached to it. Begun in 1514, it was the outward and visible sign of the worldly success of Thomas Wolsey, the Ipswich butcher's son who became a Cardinal and the most powerful man in England after King Henry VIII. He needed a residence within easy reach of London but remote from the

Hampton Court

dirt and disease of that unhealthy city. He apparently employed the most eminent physicians and even called in doctors from Italy to select the most healthy spot within twenty miles of London. Their choice fell on the old manor house of Hampton, a few miles upstream from the King's palace at Richmond. Nothing was too grand or lavish in its building – 300 rooms, maintained, it is said, by a staff of 5,000. In 1527, when the peace treaty was signed ending the war with France, the Cardinal entertained the French ambassador and his retinue of four hundred at Hampton Court.

Such ostentatious wealth and position was bound to incite Henry's envy and jealousy and two years later Wolsey was out of favour with the King and had been stripped of rank and position. He tried to curry favour with his former patron by presenting the palace to the King as a gift – but it was too late. In 1530 poor Thomas was arrested on a charge of high treason but died in mysterious circumstances before he could be brought to trial. 'If I had served my God as well as I have served the King,' he is reported to have said near the end, 'he would not have given me all these grey hairs!'

It is no surprise that Wolsey's ghost has been seen at Hampton Court but he did leave it rather late to put in an appearance. The first recorded sighting was as recently as 1966 during a son et lumière performance. The Cardinal's figure was seen under one of the archways by a member of the audience who assumed he was part of the show. The figure has been seen again a couple of times since – but where had he been for the intervening four centuries?

Several of Henry VIII's collection of wives duly have walk-on parts at Hampton Court Palace. Anne Boleyn's ghost was apparently seen frequently during the nineteenth century although she has been more shy since. Wearing a blue dress she used to be seen gliding along the same corridors that she used to walk as Queen. One witness, a servant who saw her looking downcast and disconsolate, recognised her from her portrait that hung there. Other reported sightings concern tragic Jane Seymour, Henry's next wife, who bore the long-awaited male heir but who died a week later. She appears on 12 October, the anniversary of baby Edward's birth. Dressed in white, she has been seen wandering around Clock Court and in the Silver Stick Gallery near the Queen's Apartments. She carries a lighted taper, the flame of which never flickers.

Catherine Howard, Henry's fifth wife, is perhaps the most terrifying manifestation and the famous Haunted Gallery is named because of her activities. Her fall from grace was swift and devastating. At Christmas 1540 this teenage bride had been showered with gifts by her besotted fifty-year-old husband – diamonds, pearls and rubies to excess, castles, lordships and manors, and she revelled in her sudden wealth and good fortune.

But Catherine was, by all accounts, a sexually promiscuous and energetic young woman whose physical needs the bloated Henry was not able to satisfy for long. Soon stories were circulating of the young Queen's many paramours. He at first would not believe them but when the truth became undeniable Henry wept, giving way to blubbering self-pity then wrathful anger.

Catherine was accused of having affairs with Thomas Culpepper, a gentleman of the privy chamber, and even with her cousin, Francis Dereham and she was arrested. Escaping from her guards, she dashed down the gallery towards the chapel where Henry was at his prayers, 'praying for her soul' it is said!

Held back, she pounded on the chapel door with her fists and shrieked for her husband to be merciful. But Henry pretended to be absorbed in his private communication with the Almighty and did not respond. Other accounts say that the King was in fact out hunting at the time. Catherine was taken back to her rooms and thence to the Tower of London where she was executed on 13 February 1542. Ever since, her screams have echoed from the Haunted Gallery where she is seen, dressed in white with long hair flying in the breeze, reliving her hysterical appeals for forgiveness. Some witnesses have claimed to have seen her in the gardens on summer evenings.

THE PRINCE'S NURSE

It is not just Henry's queens or the Cardinal that haunt Hampton Court. One of the strangest and best authenticated tales of all concerns young Prince Edward's nursemaid, Mistress Sybil Penn. Her job had not been an enviable one. She nursed through infancy and childhood this sickly young boy on whom so much depended. The story goes that for hours on end

St Mary's church, Hampton, where Sybil Penn's memorial is located.

she would treadle away on her spinning wheel whilst cradling Edward in her arms.

When the boy became King Edward VI in 1547, succeeding Henry VIII, he showed his affection for Mistress Sybil by giving her rooms at Hampton Court for the rest of her life and making sure she had enough money to live on. After Edward's early death in 1553 his sisters, Mary and Elizabeth, who succeeded him in turn, both maintained these arrangements. It must have been one of the few things that they agreed upon.

In November 1562 Sybil died of smallpox and was buried, not at Hampton Court, but in the parish church of St Mary's in the village of Hampton, a mile to the west and on the Middlesex bank of the Thames. Here she stayed undisturbed until 1829 when the old church was demolished and replaced with the Gothic-style building that we see today. Sybil's grave was disturbed and her tomb was somewhat awkwardly placed in the entrance lobby. Although most of her remains were reburied with due reverence, it was alleged that some of her bones were taken away by villagers or workmen as souvenirs.

Not surprisingly, Sybil took exception to this. Very soon afterwards her ghost was seen back in her old apartments at Hampton Court. Her spinning wheel and her voice were heard coming from behind a wall in the south west corner of the palace. Servants were terrified by the feeling of a cold hand on their faces while they slept nearby. Their complaints were investigated and a sealed room was found, containing an old spinning wheel and other items that dated from the Tudor period.

Some people saw her and described a tall gaunt figure in a long grey dress and close-fitting cap. One witness was a royal resident, Princess Frederica of Hanover, who had previously never heard of Sybil Penn, but found herself face to face with her in one of the corridors, to her considerable alarm. Soldiers on duty at the palace also reported seeing her and one unfortunate sentry on duty in 1881 apparently deserted his post after seeing her passing through a wall! He too is said to have been a newcomer, unaware of the story, yet his description of the apparition tallied exactly with the effigy on Sybil's tomb in Hampton Church!

AN ODD ASSORTMENT

The whole of Hampton Court seems to be alive with supernatural figures! Sir Christopher Wren, who was occupied during the last five years of his life with the remodelling of the palace for William III, has been seen at the nearby Old Court House many times on 26 February, the anniversary of his death. The same building is said to be home to a young boy, about eight years old, with shoulder-length fair hair and dressed in black velvet, with white hose and silver buckled shoes. This romantic vision is believed to have been a page boy in the time of Charles II. He was seen by guests at a party during the 1930s, walking across the lawn to the house, going up some steps and going through a door that no longer existed. It must have been quite a party!

The 'presence' of two seventeenth-century soldiers was experienced nearly two hundred years later by Lady Hillyard in her appartments overlooking

Fountain Court. This lady objected most strongly to finding two young men in her rooms and also to the rapping sounds on the panelling but nothing was done about her complaints. Then, a few years later in 1871, two workmen were laying drains outside in Fountain Court and found two skeletons buried under the paving stones. Investigations suggested at the time that they were the remains of soldiers from the time of William III, although this is now discounted by most experts. They were given proper Christian burial and thereafter Lady Hillyard was troubled no more.

Down by the Landing Stage, once the berth for royal barges, the indistinct form of yet another woman in white has been observed, according to ghost investigator Peter Underwood. He tells how a party of anglers fishing from the opposite bank witnessed her appearance, as did a number of visitors to the palace. It is said that she is the ghost of the unfortunate victim of an unhappy love affair, vainly waiting for the return of the lover who had abandoned her. Sadly, he never did return and she committed suicide by jumping from her apartment window into a false moat where she drowned in a sea of mud. Under the circumstances, it might be more appropriate if she appeared as the woman in brown – that would be more original, but perhaps less romantic!

A story from 1907 tells of a night in February when a policeman on duty at the main gate saw a group of people approaching along Ditton Walk. From their evening dress he assumed that the group of two gentlemen and eight ladies were returning on foot from a party and heading for their grace and favour lodgings in the palace. They seemed to be laughing and conversing but strangely the officer could hear no sound apart from the sensual rustling of the ladies' dresses. He turned to open the gate for them but when he looked back they had changed course and were now walking in the Kingston direction, with the two gentlemen leading them in a line. Then they vanished and although the policeman, an experienced officer with twenty years' service, made a thorough search, he found nothing.

Just before Christmas 2003 newspapers reported that a mysterious pale figure dressed in a long black coat had been caught by CCTV cameras tampering with a set of fire doors. One of the security staff was quoted as saying 'it is incredibly spooky because the face just didn't look human…'

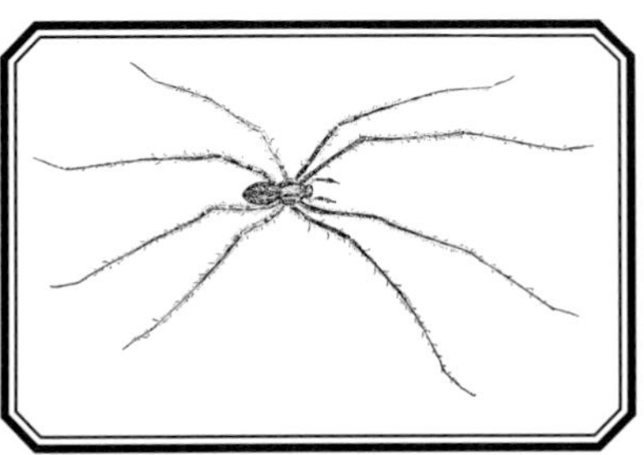

Drawing by Herbert Railton from A Short History of Hampton Court (1929).

The image on the film did look rather sinister but Professor Richard Wiseman, a psychology researcher from Hertfordshire University, was sceptical. 'It is either a publicity stunt, which I doubt,' he said, 'or a member of the public thinking they were being helpful by shutting the doors.'

Daily Telegraph reader Michael Bailey of Grayshott in Hampshire pointed out that 'real ghosts don't shut doors; they walk effortlessly through doors that are already firmly shut and locked.' Columnist Alexander Chancellor, writing in the same newspaper, commented that in his experience 'it is difficult to find anybody at Hampton Court who is not in period dress. Henry VIII's Great Hall swarms with men in doublets and codpieces and women in farthingales, prancing to the rhythms of the pavane or the galliard. The kitchens are staffed by Tudor servants in baggy trousers and floppy hats, keeping watch over mounds of plastic Tudor pork pies. This is all misguidedly designed to give the visitor the authentic Tudor experience. So it would be odd if one of these buffoons were not caught at some time on a CCTV camera.' 'I found this comment very insulting at the time' a senior member of staff wrote to me some months later'. 'All the customed staff are university graduates. The only buffoon is the idiot that wrote the article.'

Probably not a ghost, but creepier than most, is the cardinal spider – Britain's largest native species – said to be found only here.

Ernest Law in his 1929 *Short History of Hampton Court* describes how 'this enormous creature, with its fat reddish-brown body and its enormous jointed hairy legs, often attains the size of five inches in width and, when crawling about a bedroom at night, will startle even persons of tolerably composed nerves'. He goes on, 'It is alleged to be a kind of spider peculiar to Wolsey's palace and to be in some mysterious way connected with his disastrous fate, destined ever to haunt the scene of his former greatness.'

For some, this will be the most frightening thing in the book!

•Wraiths Along the River•

Dead Poet's Society

St Mary's church, Twickenham

Heroes and kings, your distance keep:
In peace let one poor poet sleep;
Who never flattered folks like you:
Let Horace blush, and Virgil too.

So read the lines on the memorial to Alexander Pope in St Mary's church at Twickenham. A modest man, he asked in his will to be carried to his grave by six of the poorest men of the parish, each of whom was to be given a suit of grey cloth.

Pope went with his parents to live in Twickenham in 1719 and died there in 1744. That he loved his home by the Thames in rural Middlesex can be judged by what he wrote of it: 'Our river glitters beneath an unclouded sun at the same time that its banks retain the verdure of the showers. Our gardens are offering their first nosegays. Our trees, like new acquaintances brought happily together, are stretching their arms to meet each other, and growing nearer and nearer every hour.'

Sadly this peaceable man was not allowed to sleep in peace as he wished. In 1830 his grave was desecrated and his skull removed from the coffin. The skull then apparently came into the possession of Johan Spurzheim, a noted phrenologist, who is said to have shown it to friends.

Perhaps the heads of poets were believed to have a distinctive shape and were therefore thought to be of scientific interest but, whatever the reason, this sacrilege did not go down too well with poor Alexander. His ghost was then seen on numerous occasions limping down the aisle of St Mary's, and also in the churchyard, raving and complaining. Presumably – and quite justifiably – he wanted his head back.

His ghost has not been seen for many years but his halting footsteps have been heard quite recently in the church, and his voice faintly demands the return of his skull.

Just downstream at Isleworth there is the strange story of the ghost that is haunting the wrong building!

Kilmorey House was built in the eighteenth-century for the Earl of Kilmorey, a noted eccentric, although he never occupied it. Next door, Gordon House, was named after Lord Frederick Gordon, but, just to make things confusing, was occupied by Lord Kilmorey. The fine gardens were believed to have been laid out under the supervision of King William IV.

Kilmorey House is said to be visited by the ghost of the old Earl despite the fact that he never lived there, dying before the house was ready. Perhaps he was determined to move in anyway but it does seem thoroughly in keeping with his reputation for eccentricity to be haunting the wrong house.

There is said to be another Isleworth ghost – that of a girl murdered in a barge early in the nineteenth century. Whether the two ghosts have ever met is not recorded.

Terrors at Twickenham

Security men at major sports stadiums like Twickenham have to be tough. Not much is likely to worry them, but according to stadium tour guide, Phil Mead, there are some who are convinced that there is a ghost at the home of English rugby!

One of the security staff's jobs is to go around late at night making sure that lights, computers, etc. have been turned off. It was two o'clock in the morning on the eve of an international and one of the guards, significantly nicknamed 'Fearless' Phil Harris, was going round on level three, starting at the south-east corner. When he arrived at the south-west corner he was surprised to see the lights on in the Obolensky restaurant area. Undaunted he went in and turned them off.

The tables in the restaurant were already set up for a function prior to the international. As Phil turned the lights off the cutlery on the tables started to rattle. He turned them on again and was shocked to find that during the brief period of darkness all two hundred chairs had been stacked on the tables. A nice trick if you can do it – think of the time you would save!

He told the strange story to a colleague, Matt Smith, who naturally did not believe him, so Phil invited him to join him on his nocturnal tour of the stadium. Just to be on the safe side they took with them Pudsey, a tough Staffordshire bull terrier.

All went well until they got to level three and Pudsey refused to get out of the lift! He struggled to get free as if his life depended on it. Leaving the whimpering animal behind they walked purposefully through the darkness to the restaurant. It was then that they became aware of a sudden and inexplicable drop in temperature. Their breath condensed and hung menacingly in the air. They retreated hastily, picking up Pudsey on their way. Matt was no longer laughing.

On another tour of duty in the small hours the now not-so-fearless Phil was in the Royal Box and, as a good security man should, he shone his powerful torch around him, sweeping towards the deserted Obolensky restaurant. Caught in the beam as it swept past he saw two faces looking back at him from the restaurant. He swung the torch back – only to see the two faces move away in different directions. Bravely, fearless after all, he returned to the restaurant but found nothing – except that distinctive drop in temperature!

Other members of the security staff confirm there is something strange about the Obolensky restaurant. Stuart Doyle said that he always feels uncomfortable walking through there and relates a tale told to him by 'Big Jim', another aptly-named guard, who from the control centre saw a television still on late at night – only to find when he went round to investigate that there were no sets left switched on at all!

There is a story that a worker was killed in an accident during the construction of the East Stand which includes the Obolensky restaurant but the stadium authorities deny this. The restaurant is named after Prince Alexander Obolensky who was born in St Petersburg in 1916. The family was related to the Tsar and, probably prudently, fled the Russian Revolution the following year. They settled in England and young Alexander had a public school education at Trent College and went up to Brasenose College, Oxford. He gained a Rugby Blue and his performance for the University XV against the New Zealand All Blacks won him a place in the England team that played New Zealand two weeks later. Ross Hamilton, the Library Officer at Twickenham, told me that Obolensky scored 'two wonderful tries' in England's 13–0 win, their first ever victory against the All Blacks.

Obolensky won three other caps for England in 1936 and seemed destined for a long and glorious career in the game. Tragically, he was killed on 29 March 1940 in Suffolk while training to be an RAF pilot. Could it be his ghost that haunts Twickenham?

The King's Mistress

When a woman whose physical attributes once charmed powerful and generous men loses her looks and patrons, her end is sad indeed. Walpole House on Chiswick Mall is believed to be haunted by the unhappy spirit of just such a lady.

Barbara Villiers was already mistress of the Earl of Chesterfield when she caught the eye of the exiled Charles, soon to be restored to the throne as Charles II. Described as 'full in figure, lovely in complexion and radiant in her youth', she was already married but her husband, Roger Palmer, was 'a dutiful and self-effacing Royalist' – which in the circumstances was just as well.

On the day in 1660 when Charles entered London in a triumphant procession there were great festivities and he made a gracious speech at Whitehall but a thanksgiving service in Westminster Abbey was cancelled and, it is said, the King slipped quietly away to spend the first night of his Restoration with Barbara. This says something about his priorities perhaps. An Earldom was found for the pliant Roger Palmer, making Barbara, Lady Castlemaine. She became a spoilt plaything who wanted her own way. She bore the King three sons but, of course, as they were illegitimate, they could not inherit. English history would have been very different had they been able to!

But by 1671 Charles had many other mistresses and Barbara was losing her attraction for him, even though she was still only in her twenties. He would no longer put up with her rages and her greed. Her extravagance became legendary – she would appear at the theatre wearing jewellery worth £30,000 and could lose as much in a night at the gambling tables of smart salons. When Charles gave her the great Tudor palace of Nonsuch she quickly began to dismantle it and sell the contents – an asset-stripper in fact.

Barbara did nothing for Charles' dwindling popularity but he did not desert her entirely. He created her Duchess of Cleveland and acknowledged her latest daughter as his own. In fact the baby was not his. With the King occupied elsewhere, Barbara was taking other lovers and it was widely believed that the real father was John Churchill, who was to win renown in a later reign as the country's greatest soldier, becoming the Duke of Marlborough. She could still pick the rising young men!

To have lived the high life in such style and then live on to become a friendless old woman was indeed a cruel fate. She became afflicted with dropsy and, according to a contemporary source, 'swelled to a monstrous bulk' and it is this substantial spectre that is said to haunt Walpole House, her home for the last two years of her life. It is a lovely gracious house on the waterfront with views across the sweep of the river towards Hammersmith – but it can have given her little pleasure. The tip-tap of her high heels is heard on the stairs and her mournful face seen pressed against a window. Hands clasped in despair, she pleads for the return of her lost beauty.

The house later became a private school and Thackeray came here as a small boy. It is believed that he based Miss Pinkerton's Academy in Vanity Fair on Walpole House.

Boston House. (Hounslow Cultural and Community Services)

A nearby ghost is that of Lady Boston at Boston House in Chiswick Square. The square today has lost much of its charm, positioned as it is right by the Hogarth Roundabout and flyover on the arterial road out of London but Boston House is set back from the din of the dual carriageway and still looks grand and dignified.

The story goes that when her husband discovered her affair with a neighbour, General Lord Fairfax (Chiswick ghosts have all the right social connections!), he murdered her and took her body down a dark passage which led from the house to the river. The body was, however, washed up by the tide a few days later and buried with great secrecy in a corner of the garden. There have been sightings of a woman in a long dress with hands outstretched and with a look of terror on her face, recalling the horror of her murder.

Another version has Lady Boston writing secret letters to Fairfax and arranging to leave the house by the back door and meeting her lover at a cypress tree in the garden. The ghost is seen following this clandestine route but always disappearing when she reaches the tree.

Early in the twentieth century the Chiswick Polish Company (floor polish, not Eastern Europeans!) occupied the house. The company built an annexe containing a staff restaurant that went right over Lady Boston's grave. Company workers in the 1920s are said to have seen the ghost.

One internet site tells this same story but locates it at Boston Manor in Brentford but this must be too far from the river. According to this account, the skeleton of a woman was found buried in the grounds of Boston Manor by the nuns of a Roman Catholic order who occupied the house before the Second World War.

Also in Chiswick – the Old Burlington in Church Street, now a private residence, was an alehouse back in Elizabethan times. The building dates from the sixteenth century and, with its overhanging upper storey and exposed timbers, is probably the oldest house in Chiswick. It is said to be haunted by a ghost with the less-than-supernatural name of Percy. Described as 'good-natured and harmless' and dressed in a wide-brimmed hat and long cloak, he is thought to have been a highwayman. I'm bound to say that, if he was good-natured and harmless in life, he cannot have been a particularly successful highwayman!

Old Burlington, Chiswick.

I was hoping to have a drink in the Old Burlington to see whether any of the locals could vouch for the tale. Sadly, it is a pub no longer although it retains its attractive jettied timber frontage. It is almost in the shadow of St Nicholas church where the sad Duchess of Cleveland was laid to rest.

A more sinister occult presence in Chiswick than dear old Percy was reported from Esmond Road in July 1956. A couple and their thirteen-year-old son were driven from their home by coins flying through the air, an onslaught that began the week the family moved into the house. As so often in the case of poltergeists, the strange phenomena seemed to centre around the child. Wherever he went in the house, pennies, razor-blades, clothes-pegs and even a spanner are said to have hurtled through the air alarmingly. 'It was as if he was magnetised', his mother told reporters.

A priest performed a service of exorcism in the house and the poltergeist activity ceased.

The Artist's Models

Chiswick Police Station in Linden Gardens is built on the site of the former Linden House, home of an unsuccessful nineteenth-century painter called Thomas Wainwright, and is haunted by

Linden House, Chiswick. (Hounslow Cultural and Community Services)

Wainwright's mother-in-law, Mrs Abercrombie. Their story was the subject of a criminal investigation at the time, involving as it does, allegations of fraud and murder.

Thomas Wainwright had been born in the house and, after serving in the Army, he married a girl called Eliza. They lived in London, where Wainwright was seeking to establish himself as a painter. He used his mother-in-law and sister-in-law as his models. This must have saved the expense of paying someone else to pose for him but his finances were still pretty rocky.

By 1822 he was desperate and he attempted a scam by forging signatures in order to obtain money left in trust by his grandfather. This failed but he then struck lucky when his uncle died leaving him Linden House. The inheritance was not as big financially as he was hoping for – and perhaps needed – but he moved back to Linden House with the three women in his life.

Very soon afterwards Mrs Abercrombie became strangely ill. She suffered convulsions and soon died of a stomach complaint. Within a week the sister-in-law was also dead of the same thing. This looked suspicious and rather too convenient for the feckless artist and he was arrested and sent to Newgate Prison to await trial for murder. There was not, it seems, enough evidence for a successful prosecution. However, Wainwright was found guilty of fraud and transported to Australia.

Linden House eventually became a fire station and it was at that time that Mrs Abercrombie made her ghostly appearance, usually in the basement but also on the third floor. Footsteps were heard during the night but if anyone turned on the light the sounds would stop abruptly.

THE MURDER OF THE HAMMERSMITH GHOST

Late in 1803 strange, mysterious happenings began to occur in Hammersmith. There were reports of a ghostly white figure haunting the graveyard. Rumour followed rumour and the ghost was said to be that of a local man who had committed suicide by cutting his own throat.

One night, just before Christmas, a woman – perhaps foolishly under the circumstances – took a short cut past the graveyard. It was about ten o'clock. She saw a spectral white figure rising up from behind a tombstone. She tried to run but the ghost came after her, caught up with her and, to her horror, wrapped its white arms around her. Not surprisingly, this was too much for her shattered nerves and the poor lady fainted.

When she did not return as expected, worried neighbours went out into the darkened streets to look for her. They found her wandering aimlessly around the graveyard in a state of extreme shock. They took her home and put her to bed but the trauma had been too much for her and the unfortunate woman died.

The search was on in earnest for what was now widely known as the 'Hammersmith Ghost'. Some believed that the explanation could only lie in the realm of the supernatural but others, more prosaically, believed that some flesh and blood prankster was to blame, A vigilante group, in those days called a watch committee, was formed and brave folk hid around the graveyard hoping to catch him at it. They met with little success and the apparitions continued. Whether spirit or practical joker, the Hammersmith Ghost was leading them all a merry dance.

Francis Smith, a young excise officer, living in lodgings nearby was one of the watch committee. On the night of 3 January 1804 he was in the White Hart, one of Hammersmith's many pubs, and the conversation turned to the ghost and the total failure of the vigilantes to stop its activities. Emboldened by drink, Smith decided that he would sort the thing out once and for all. He returned home, got his trusty old fowling piece and, without consulting any of his colleagues on the watch committee, went to lie in wait for the ghost in Black Lion Lane. The night was dark and the visibility poor.

At eleven o'clock Smith was making his way between the high dark hedges that bordered the lane. As he nervously crossed Limekiln Lane he suddenly saw an indistinct white figure approaching him

'Stop, who goes there?' he called out, in the best tradition of sentries the world over. There was no reply.

'Speak out or I'll shoot!' Still no reply as the white figure came ever onward. Smith fired – and the ball hit the figure in the mouth, knocking it backwards and causing it to crumple to the ground with a most unspirit-like thump. It twitched momentarily and then lay still. Francis Smith approached the fallen figure and, to his horror, recognised it as a local man, Thomas Millwood. He was well known in the district as a jobbing bricklayer and was dressed in his usual working clothes – white trousers, white apron and white jacket, covered in a pale powdering of dust from his day's work.

Hearing the shot, a group of men had come out to investigate. They found the incoherent figure of Francis Smith, who immediately confessed to what he had done. The police were called and Smith was taken into custody at Bow Street police station, from where he was taken to Newgate Prison to await trial.

The trial began at the Old Bailey on Friday 13 January 1804, an ill-omened date, and transcripts can still be seen in the official records. The court heard evidence of how Hammersmith had been gripped for weeks with fear and terror as a result of the frequent sightings of the 'ghost' in the vicinity of the churchyard, of the events of the fateful night of 3 January and of the previous good character of Francis Smith.

Despite attempts to get it reduced to manslaughter, the judges were insistent that the only possible charge the jury could consider was murder. They had no option but to find Smith guilty. It was with despair and foreboding that the prisoner heard the death sentence passed and there cannot have been anyone in court – apart from the unfortunate Mr Millwood's family – who did not feel sympathy for the pallid 29-year-old Francis Smith at that moment.

How his hopes must have risen when Lord Chief Justice Baron then announced that, in view of the special and tragic circumstances in this case, he would be referring the case to the king. That same evening news came of a full pardon on condition that Smith serve a one year term of imprisonment. I imagine he must have been happy and relieved to do so.

The Black Lion, Hammersmith.

But what of Thomas Millwood? As a local man, he must have been aware of the alarm that the sightings of the white figure in the graveyard had been causing. Did it not occur to him that he could possibly have been the cause of all the agitation? Why didn't he take the obvious precaution of wearing a dark overcoat?

Unless, of course, there had been a real ghost a-haunting in Hammersmith all along!

Ghost hunters wishing to recreate the atmosphere of two hundred years ago would find it difficult today. The Great West Road carves its way through, separating most of Hammersmith from the river. Black Lion Lane is insensitively cut in two right by St Peter's church but does just give a hint of what the streets that Millwood walked must have been like. The Black Lion pub, attractively situated close to the river, retains memories of the story, outlined on a board outside.

The Woman Sewn Up in a Sack

Beavor Lodge at Hammersmith was a plain-looking eighteenth-century house whose gardens ran down to the Thames. It was demolished in 1928 but in its day it was noted for a varied collection of ghosts.

In the early 1870s the property was acquired by Sir William Richmond and his wife. Almost immediately the family became aware of strange noises downstairs. Windows would be shaken in the small hours and doors opened as if of their own accord. There were sounds of someone sobbing and sighing. Lady Richmond reported 'the sound of stitching in the room next to my bedroom as if some hard and coarse work were being done, and then the sound of something being dragged across the floor. I got to have a feeling of being watched, which was most uncomfortable.'

One afternoon in October 1875, while reading to her children, Lady Richmond rang for the parlour maid. When the door opened she saw an unfamiliar female figure, dressed in grey diaphanous material. The apparition walked to the table behind the children, then turned towards the door and, moving towards it, seemed to dissolve away.

Naturally, Mrs Richmond did not say anything about this experience to the servants (heaven forbid!) but within the next couple of months two of them saw the same thing. One was so upset that she immediately resigned her post. The following year the Richmonds' six-year-old daughter, who also had been kept in ignorance of what her mother had seen, was terrified in the night when she awoke to see 'a wicked-looking old grey woman at the end of my bed, staring at me with evil eyes'. This time the figure had disappeared into the floor with a loud noise. Things seemed to be getting more serious: the next thing to happen was that Lady Richmond had her hair pulled by the ghost.

The Grey Lady was also seen in the garden, especially on a particular seat beneath a pear tree. On one occasion, it was claimed, she was seen by two people – one of them a bishop – from different parts of the garden. They compared notes on what they had seen and their descriptions tallied exactly.

Sir William himself, alone in the house with his dog, was startled to hear the dog growling as the handle of the door shook and, although the door remained closed, the figure of a woman, dressed as a nun this time, her face concealed by a veil, stood on the threshold and then disappeared.

Investigations suggested two conflicting explanations for the hauntings. One theory said that counterfeiters had once used the house and that, after a woman accidentally came upon them and their criminal activity, they killed her by sewing her up in a sack and bundling her into the Thames. This would account for the strange noises heard by Mrs Richmond, who was previously unaware of the story.

The Grey Lady was finally put to rest after a séance at which those present were told that the ghost was in fact the spirit of a nun who had given birth to a baby. To avoid the inevitable disgrace she had murdered the baby and buried the body in the meadow opposite Beavor Lodge. Perhaps Sir William and his wife saw different ghosts!

Associated with the Grey Lady's appearances were the so-called 'Roystering Beavorites'. People sleeping in the bedrooms would be disturbed at night by the sounds of loud voices after midnight. It sounded like a lively party breaking up and there were sounds of coach doors slamming as they prepared to bear the partygoers off into the night. If anyone ever got up to investigate, the noises ceased and there was no sign next morning that anything had been amiss.

It seems that after the séance Beavor Lodge reverted to the tranquil state it had been in before the Richmonds moved in but it is said that on his deathbed in 1921 the aged Sir William pointed to a dark corner of the room and croaked 'There stands the Grey Lady!'

Railway Sleepers

The wild-eyed figure on the level crossing walked on oblivious as the train came steaming up behind him. Too late the driver saw him out of the round spectacle glass of the tank engine. Too late the brakes were applied, the elderly engine wheels screaming and sliding along the rails. There was a sickening thump and the man lay dying beside the single line.

Camille Pissarro was unique among the French Impressionists in his interest in painting the suburbs of London. Many French artists visited the city in the latter years of the nineteenth-century but the few travelled to the outer suburbs as Pissarro did.

Early in 1897 Camille's son Lucien and his wife Esther moved to 62 Bath Road, Bedford Park, Hammersmith. The house had a view of open fields on one side and a single-track railway on the other. There was a gated level crossing controlled by a signal box at the point where the railway crossed Bath Road.

Pissarro visited his son and daughter-in-law and while there painted a picture of a goods train chuffing towards the Bath Road crossing. The painting is now in a private collection but was exhibited at the *Pissarro in London* exhibition at the National Gallery during the summer of 2003.

The railway was a rather hopeless enterprise. Running from South Acton station on the North London Railway, it meandered in a slow loop around Bedford Park to a terminus vaguely near the river and called Hammersmith & Chiswick station, which was in fact not in either place. It can never have

The Bath Road level crossing. (John Gillham)

paid its way and even as early as 1897 trains were infrequent and poorly patronised.

Lucien and Esther's home became the focus of a glittering group of political radicals, artists and writers. Among them was a brooding Russian known as Stepniak, an infamous anarchist who had been arrested and imprisoned several times in his homeland for his dangerous political activities. Fearing more persecution he came to London and became a member of the Pissarros' menage at Bath Road. Another member of the group was the children's writer Edith Nesbit who was later to immortalise Stepniak as the mysterious Russian exile in her book *The Railway Children*.

It is said that Stepniak had trained himself to withstand intensive interrogation by his captors by shutting out all external distractions from his mind. A useful talent in an overcrowded Russian jail perhaps but sadly fatal on a level crossing when a train was approaching.

Having said that, given the infrequency of trains on the little railway that crossed Bath Road and the slow speed at which they travelled, Stepniak was spectacularly unlucky to have been hit by one and killed. Is it possible that this was no accident but a cleverly-staged political assassination?

The railway was closed and dismantled nearly half a century ago and there is no trace of the level-crossing in Bath Road – but on a dark winter's night local people may still hear the shrill warning whistle of the engine, the screaming of the locked wheels along the track, the cry of alarm in a strange tongue and that awful thump as iron and steel meet flesh and bone!

A particularly unfortunate passenger is said to haunt Ickenham station on the Metropolitan Line near Uxbridge. In 1951 an electrician working at the station in the small hours when there were no trains running was alarmed to see a middle-aged woman standing watching him. She gestured that he should follow her, led him along the platform and down the exit stairway. As she reached the bottom step she vanished. Several London Transport workers have seen her at various times. The ghost is believed to be that of a woman who, many years ago, fell from the platform onto the live rail and was electrocuted.

Another station with an eerie atmosphere is Highgate, also on the Northern Line. The tube platforms are underground but above them in a densely wooded cutting are the remains of the former surface station. This lay claustrophobically between two pairs of single-track tunnels. Sometime early in the twentieth century a man is said to have walked into one of these tunnels and been killed by an oncoming train. His ghost is reputed to haunt the deserted station still – people who have ventured onto the platforms have complained of the feeling that they are being watched.

It is a strange forgotten place. It was rebuilt in 1941 for the planned operation of Northern Line tube trains along the branch through Highgate to Muswell Hill and Alexandra Palace. The electrification scheme was halted by the war and never restarted. In July 1954 the Alexandra Palace branch was closed to

Ickenham station.

passengers, the last goods train ran ten years later. Yet folk living near to the closed line at Highgate and Crouch End claim that on occasions they have heard the sounds of trains at night.

Part of the route is now open as a footpath, although Highgate station itself is not accessible. The route ends in the shadow of Alexandra Palace. When this grotesque structure was built in the 1860s a group of gypsies was forcibly removed from their encampment on the top of the hill. Enraged, they put a curse on the place: 'May death and destruction befall this place and everything associated with it!'

Within a year the palace had burnt down in mysterious circumstances and, although rebuilt, it never really lived up to the high hopes of its promoters.

AND THE GHOST CAME TOO ...

The inhabitants at a house on the West Brompton Road in the early years of the twentieth century were disturbed at night by the sound of knocking, mysterious footsteps, the ringing of bells and the sight of a grey draped figure, hands clasped as if in prayer. It moved with a strange gliding motion or stopped and stared fixedly at any onlooker. Shadowy and unsubstantial though it appeared, there was yet a luminous glow emanating from it which was impossible to ignore. It never moved its hands and never spoke. It never made a sound, except for one curious occasion when, according to one witness, it dropped a parcel or package that it was carrying.

Alarming as it might seem to the reader, the inhabitants of the house did not find it so. For seven years this inoffensive apparition continued to make appearances at irregular intervals. It was not out of fear that the family eventually decided to move to another house in the same area.

Yet the move made things a whole lot worse – for their supernatural guest moved with them and the disruption to his routine seemed to have robbed him of his peaceable nature. Not only did the family see the same shadowy figure and hear the same noises but now doors were banged where no doors existed, there were sounds like metal trays being clashed together, noises of furniture being moved around, the constant tramp of footsteps up and down the corridors, matches being struck in the darkness and loud heartbreaking sighs.

On Christmas Day the figure was seen by one of the daughters, standing first on the staircase and then at the foot of her bed. A boy, ill in bed at the time, was so affected by what was happening around him that his condition worsened and he died three weeks later. For some days before his death the disturbances in the house were as bad as they had ever been, yet after a while the hauntings finally subsided and the family – notwithstanding its tragic loss of a son – was not disturbed again.

How to Tame a Poltergeist

Back in 1953 the impressively-named Nandor Fodor and Hereward Carrington published an important, if somewhat indigestible, study of poltergeist phenomena. One of the cases they described concerned a cottage in Chelsea inhabited by a Miss Whalan.

The cottage was 300 years old, dating from a time when Chelsea was just a riverside village in rural Middlesex, but it would seem that it was the unfortunate Miss Whalan herself who was the focus of the strange happenings that she endured. These included footsteps and objects suddenly moving or flying through the air. According to another person living in the house, the activity ceased while Miss Whalan was in hospital for an operation, only to start up again on her return.

Mr Fodor, who investigated the case, wrote, 'I was convinced that the creepy atmosphere of the old house lent itself to an unconscious projection and dramatisation of one's own conflicts into ghostly manifestations.' Translated into English, I think this means, 'It was all in her mind'!

He went on, 'I decided to ignore the dynamics of the reported happenings and informed Miss Whalan of my considered opinion that she was haunted by her own past.' (In other words, 'It's your own fault, dear.')

Perhaps somewhat condescendingly, he explained to her that the footsteps represented 'the arrival of the message' and that the disappearance of objects 'a troublesome complex that you must attend to'. I must remember that the next time I mislay something vital.

Miss Whalen must have been an obedient and trusting soul. She seems to have accepted this explanation immediately. 'Deep within herself she felt that she was in some way involved in the phenomena,' Fodor wrote. In the book he describes working through her dreams with her and bringing out the various 'repressed beliefs and history' that were causing her problems.

And, as if by magic, the hauntings ceased.

•Horrors Near Heathrow•

An Unexpected Guest

The Priory ruins. (Hounslow Cultural and Community Services)

All Saints' Church in Hounslow High Street is a lively modern church and stands near the site of the medieval Trinitarian priory at Hounslow. The priory was established early in the thirteenth century and in 1296 granted the right to hold a weekly market and an annual fair. It held land in various local parishes but was never a particularly wealthy or nationally influential establishment. It did, however, play a part in a mysterious incident which was not resolved for over four hundred years and which may perhaps have supernatural connotations.

One evening in March 1413, shortly after the death of Henry IV in the Jerusalem Chamber at Westminster, the monks were at supper in the refectory when there came a loud knocking at the outer door – a man claiming the ancient right of monastic hospitality and sanctuary for the night. The wild-eyed figure admitted by the gatekeeper and brought to the prior was Clement Maydestone, and he had a strange tale to tell once his hunger and thirst were satisfied.

He was, he claimed, one of three men who had stolen the corpse of the late King and thrown it into the Thames between Barking and Gravesend whilst it was being conveyed from Westminster to Canterbury for burial. He said that the ornate chest, covered with cloth of gold, in which the body had lain, had later been carried with great pomp and ceremony – but empty – into the cathedral and subsequently buried with all appropriate reverence and ritual. The enormity of his crime had driven him mad and he implored God's forgiveness. Given the setting of the remote and darkened priory on the edge of the heath, it was an appropriately Gothic tale.

Despite the authorities' best efforts the story got out and created a sensation. The tale was told in taverns and hawked around by ballad singers and hucksters. Some believed that the ghost of the unburied monarch haunted the bleak Thames marshes crying out for Christian burial. His successor Henry V's coronation was marked by terrible blizzards that buried men, beasts and houses deep in snow, carried by furious winds that brought fear into the stoutest hearts.

But was the story true? And who was the strange wild man who had disturbed the cloistered calm of the priory? Was he real or could he have been a ghost or some strange apparition?

The rumours would not go away. Amazingly, it was not until 1832 that the matter was finally settled. In that year the tomb of Henry IV in Canterbury Cathedral was opened in the presence of the Bishop of Oxford, the Dean of Canterbury and other worthies.

The remains of King Henry were indeed found in the coffin, minutely examined, sifted over and pronounced genuine, thus finally disproving the unlikely story told by a wandering mendicant at Hounslow Priory all those centuries before. How was it that such an improbable tale, without any evidence to back it up, was believed in the first place?

Highwayman's Heath

It seems improbable that Hounslow should ever have featured in a book called *Beauties of Britain*, but it did so once – in 1816. It has to be said, however, that even then the authors, Messrs. Brayley and Britton, were less than complimentary. 'The chief dependence of the place is on the

Hounslow Heath. (Hounslow Cultural and Community Services)

immense tide of road traffic which rolls to and from the metropolis with surprising vehemence and bustle,' they wrote. 'All here wear the face of impatience and expedition. The whole population seems on the wing for removal; and assuredly the main street of Hounslow is a place from which the examiner would wish to remove with all celerity.'

Some would say that nothing has changed, but Hounslow High Street must have been a welcome sight to London-bound travellers in eighteenth-century coaching days as it meant that they had safely traversed the infamous highwayman-infested Hounslow Heath.

Tales of the dark deeds of Dick Turpin and his contemporaries were recorded in *Highwayman's Heath* by Gordon S. Maxwell, first published in 1935 and reissued in 1994. One of Mr Maxwell's stories concerns the so-called Bloody Post erected on Hounslow Heath, alongside the road to Whitton. This gruesome landmark was inscribed as follows: 'Buried here, with a stake drove through the body, is the wicked murderer John Proctor, who cut the throats of his wife and child and then poisoned himself, July 6th 1765.'

Maxwell quotes the Reverend John Evans, a clergyman who, in 1818, published a book of *Excursions*. Evans wrote of the Bloody Post that 'the sight of such an object instantly conjures up in the imagination all those cruelties which have been perpetuated on this secluded spot by wretches in the last stages of depravity. Of later years, however, the traveller has met with fewer interruptions, though we still hear, not infrequently, of robberies in that quarter during the winter season, a proof of which is exhibited by a gibbet near Bedfont, on which we saw the body of Haines, generally known as the 'Wounded Highwayman'. He was a large tall man; his irons were so constructed that his arms hung at some little distance from his body, by which means the hideous sight was rendered more terrific and impressive. The skirts of his coat waved in the wind and suggested with full force the horrible idea of a fellow creature deprived of the honours of sepulture [burial] and consigned, with every mark of execration, to the grinning scorn of public infamy.'

A magazine article published in 1845, *Musings by an Old Toll-Gate on Hounslow Heath*, gives a vivid impression of the sinister reputation the area still had then: 'You see nothing around for miles but the lonely heath, and you think

The Bell, Hounslow.

of the long winter nights when the hours of darkness hang over the silent scene. You recall the winds which blow all night long and the awful roaring of the tall trees, mingled with the heavy showers that beat upon the windows, sounding like robbers breaking through. Near at hand stands a gibbet-post where a murder was committed, and the gibbet-irons swing and creak in the wind.

'Or maybe that someone who destroyed himself is buried at the crossroads, as was the custom, and all the country-folk believe the spot is haunted, for at twelve o'clock nobody knows what he has seen. Drunken farmers on horseback have been chased and timid ploughboys have had to run for it; and the old toll-man has had to come out to one fainting, another speechless and a third with hair standing on end, and if you believe but half there was never such a spot where 'bogles' laid wait and caught you unawares. One woman's all in white and another without a head. You could never see their faces but you heard the rustle of their garments and felt the cold air as they glided by, and if you approached they vanished ... Nothing you could prove or disprove – but it is common gossip round many a country hearth in this part of Middlesex.'

Writing in 1935, Gordon Maxwell quotes another chilling tale which has no simple solution. 'Set some distance from the main highway across Hounslow Heath there stood until comparatively recently an old dwelling, half farmhouse, half inn, which was, like many others hereabouts, reputed to have been the resort of highwaymen. When it was demolished, cunningly placed behind the panelling was a cavity in the wall, which, when opened, showed a gruesome sight. Propped up against the wall, half sitting, half kneeling, was the skeleton of a man dressed in the riding attire of about 1780, with a pistol in his belt and another on the floor by him. The latter had been discharged and part of the man's skull was blown away. Fallen from the pocket of his now rotten coat were two gold watches, some rings, and a score of guineas dated 1776.

'Here evidently was all that remained of some bold gentleman of the road who, for some reason had, in a fit of despair or because he had been left to starve, blown out his brains. We learned that the old house had for many years borne the reputation of being haunted by a highwayman's ghost, the troubled spirit of one known as 'Black Will'.'

Maddeningly, Maxwell's source for this story, an anonymous nineteenth-century writer in a magazine, did not specify the exact location of the find but there are a number of Hounslow pubs, including the Bell inn and the Hussar, that claim to be haunted by the ghosts of highwaymen. At the Bell, according to a report in the *Middlesex Chronicle* in September 1988, the ghosts smashed kegs of beer (presumably to get at the contents!). Pub manager George Smith, who had taken over in 1986, told the paper that the breweries made allowances for what the ghosts spilled. 'They know it's not me siphoning off the ale because the same thing used to happen before I arrived.'

Mr Smith said that it could not be the work of flesh and blood thieves because he doubled-checked the cellar last thing every night. 'I always switch off the lights and lock the doors,' he said, 'but in the morning I find the lights on, taps from the beer barrels removed and ale flooding the floor.' His wife, Anthea, was too frightened to go down there at all.

The couple lived upstairs in the pub and often heard doors slamming in the middle of the night and glasses crashing off the shelves. Some of the pub's regulars told of a man who never bought a drink but just sat and stared around him. 'They believe he's the soul of one of the hanged highwaymen,' Mr Smith said. One of the cleaning staff even alleged that there was a ghost in the Gents' and refused to go in there but all this did not seem to deter the customers. 'They are pleased with all the spirits we have on offer,' Mr Smith said cheerfully.

Dobermans can be fierce guard dogs but one named Guinness was too terrified by what he had experienced to go back down into the cellar of the Hussar pub on the Staines Road at Hounslow Heath. 'I don't blame him for not going down there,' said landlord 'Big Al' Bradshaw. 'I know it's haunted because I've seen the ghosts. They are black shadowy figures. When I speak to them they just disappear into the wall. They make my flesh creep and I have to rush upstairs. I know they are around because the room goes very cold. They come creeping up behind me.'

Other manifestations at the Hussar included curtains ripping open when doors and windows were closed and scuffling noises late at night. Some guests staying overnight swore never to do so again after seeing a hooded highwayman at the window! Similar sightings were reported from the old Nag's Head pub in Hounslow High Street which closed on 2 January 1954. Mrs Stokes, the licensee, also claimed that her bed had been shaken violently under her by the shadowy cloaked figure. Investigators from the Society for Psychical Research suggested that the ghost might have been opposed to the impending demolition of the premises.

One inn along the High Street was alleged to have a bedroom with a secret exit into the yard through which Dick Turpin, tipped off by the landlord who had been suitably bribed, is said to have escaped into the yard as the forces of the law closed in on him. It is said that early in the twentieth century a commercial traveller expressed great interest in this romantic chamber and, despite its reputation for being haunted, asked if he could sleep there. This he did – with the result that he left by the secret exit early next morning without paying his bill!

THE LAUGHING CHILDREN

A tragic tale came from one of the junior schools in Feltham some time ago. The school is still there and it would be unfair to name it and risk upsetting its present pupils.

The school building was also used by a local youth group and one evening two of the youth leaders were alone in the building packing things away. All the group members had left and gone home. Suddenly the two leaders heard the sound of laughing children coming from somewhere in the building.

'It sounds as if some of the little blighters have gone upstairs and are running about,' said one of them, who clearly harboured no romantic ideals about the behaviour of his charges. They went to investigate, following the sound – but nothing and no-one was found.

Afterwards one of them, puzzled, asked a friend who had been a pupil at the school some years before if he knew of a possible explanation for what he had heard.

'I suppose you know that a little girl was run over in the playground and died', was the chilling reply. It appears that the child had dashed into the path of a milk float delivering to the school and had received fatal injuries.

Next week at the youth group special prayers were said for past and present members of the school. This was done without giving any hint to the members of what their leaders had experienced the previous week. They hoped that if the spirit of the little girl was still visiting her old school to play with her friends that it would now finally be laid to rest.

STILL LOOKING FOR HIS BRIEFCASE

A trespasser on the tarmac at Heathrow Airport must be the ultimate nightmare for Air Traffic Control. One evening in 1970 radar units detected what seemed to be a man walking on Runway One. The police organised a thorough search of the site, using three squad cars and a fire engine, directed to the exact spot by radio.

London Airport, 1968.

'He must be just in front of you,' the radio operator advised the searchers ... 'You must have run over him! ... He's behind you now.' There was definitely something on the radar screen but the anxious police out on the runway could see nothing. They turned round and were about to resume their search when they were informed that, according to the radar screen, they had just run over him again, but eventually, with nothing found, the search was called off. The same thing happened several times that day and the police inspector involved, Leslie Alton, later told Frank Durham, a reporter on the *Sunday Mirror*, that he had experienced incidents of extra-sensory perception before and had 'a completely open mind' about what had happened.

On 2 March 1948 a Sabena Dakota DC3 crashed in fog on Runway One, killing all twenty-two people on board. It is said that while the rescue crews searched the wreckage for possible survivors, a smartly-suited man in a bowler hat, described as being 'ex-Guards', six feet tall and in his late 40s, asked each of them in turn if they had found his briefcase. It is this man who is still occasionally seen walking on the runways by night workers and evening visitors to Heathrow, although some of them have him in cavalry twill trousers rather than a business suit.

The dreary wastelands of Heathrow Airport must be a particularly dispiriting place for a ghost to be condemned to haunt for all eternity. I hope someone finds the man's all-important briefcase so that he can continue his journey!

Another strange happening, which some link to the first story, occurred in October 1971 when cleaners at Heathrow reported that they were experiencing strange happenings on some jumbo jets. They complained that at times they felt unable to move as if being held down by something. No explanation was ever forthcoming for the phenomenon, which now seems to have ceased.

The Last Wolf of Perry Oaks

Tourists might think Perry Oaks a romantic rural-sounding name but these days it is best known as the extensive sewage works that were cleared to become the site of Heathow Airport's controversial Terminal 5. Seventy years ago, when described by Gordon Maxwell in *Highwayman's Heath*, it was just 'a few scattered cottages, a delightful old farm, some orchards and meadows … a beautiful spot. Few have ever heard of it and if you ask the average person if they know it they look at you as if you were enquiring for a place in Cumberland, or some equally far-away place, instead of one hardly a dozen miles from London.'

In 1665, somewhere in the district, Samuel Pepys got lost in the woods that gave Perry Oaks its name, recording in his famous diary: 'I went to the new post-house at Charing Cross and there got horses to Hounslow. So to Staines and there, by this time, it was dark and got a guide, who got lost in the forest, till by help of the moon I led my guide in the way again.'

The area had long been dangerous for the unwary. Wild beasts abounded. In the medieval accounts of the Manor of Harmondsworth, which included Perry Oaks, there is mention of a swineherd whose job it was to watch over the pigs in the woods to guard them against wolves.

Maxwell records the old tradition that the last wolf in England was hunted down to its death at Perry Oaks some time early in the thirteenth century. He tells a strange story, which sounds supernatural but which has more than one twist in the tale.

'One autumn afternoon,' he wrote in 1935, 'I happened to be at Perry Oaks. Though certainly now denuded of forest, it is still lonely enough for any wolf to make it its home. Twilight was fast closing into night as I sat on a field gate smoking and let my imagination run riot, trying to picture what the place must have been like in those far-off days when giant oaks covered the now-cleared ground and the traveller might meet the dreaded wolf in any forest glade. In front of me, about fifty yards across a clearing, was a clump of trees, thick enough to fade into dark shadows in the interior.

'I was looking at those trees, whose roots were hidden by a slight ground mist and their blackness rather allured me. All at once I was conscious of a rather uncanny feeling; for out of the darkness gleamed two green eyes. I watched fascinated. It was no hallucination – it was a wolf's head!

'Had my imagination been so strong as to conjure up visions? In another moment the body of the animal came into view, turning at a right-angle to the trees and making its way across the field in front. There was no mistaking that profile; the long 'lolloping' gait of a wolf is peculiar to that animal, and the jaws were open, showing the great fangs, with the tongue hanging out at one corner.

'I did not move but still gazed spellbound. There was not a sound, no footsteps were audible, but without a doubt there was the shadow of a huge grey wolf, magnified and slightly distorted by the mist. It was terribly real – and yet so unreal … Was this spirit from the past appearing on the very spot where tradition said that the last of its race in this country expired with the hunter's arrow through its quivering heart?

'If the beast had just passed across the view, and so out of sight, I might still think I had seen the ghost of England's last wolf, had not a diversion occurred that brought me to earth. A whistle sounded close by and the animal turned quickly and made towards the gate. A man emerged from the copse, his footsteps, like those of the wolf, deadened by the grass.

'The mystery was cleared up, for when the 'wolf' got near I saw what it was – a large Alsatian dog. I spoke to the owner – he was much interested and amused when I told him my story; though he lived at Stanwell he had never heard of the legend of the Last Wolf of Perry Oaks.'

Not a supernatural apparition at all then – but Mr Maxwell concluded that 'it was nevertheless a strange coincidence that the first cousin to the wolf should suddenly appear on this spot at the time my thoughts were on this subject'.

He ends his story with a report from a local newspaper published shortly afterwards: 'Four sheep were killed and thirty injured by an Alsatian dog on a farm at Heath Row; watch was kept and the dog was shot.' The spirit of the past come to haunt the present – the then-rural community of Heath Row was only a mile from Perry Oaks. 'I only hope,' Maxwell wrote, 'that it wasn't my friend, 'the wolf'.'

M FOR MYSTERY

Late one night in the autumn of 1993 a woman was driving alone along the M4, returning home to London from Reading. She was driving fast. The motorway was more or less devoid of traffic and brightly lit.

Suddenly, between junctions four and three near Heathrow Airport, she saw a figure walking towards her along the carriageway. The driver's reactions had to be swift – she swerved into the middle lane and passed within inches of the apparition at upwards of 80 miles per hour. The figure in the road just stared straight ahead and did not even flinch as the car swept past her!

It was a woman dressed in black. She seemed to be wearing a raincoat and sou'wester – but it was not raining. She was carrying a bag in each hand – and she was just walking on down the motorway towards the oncoming traffic.

The witness described the figure as 'looking like someone out of a Catherine Cookson novel'. She seemed about 60 years old, with severely-cut short hair and a bitter and haggard expression.

In her rear-view mirror the driver saw another car swerve to avoid the figure. Surely if the woman's car had broken down on the motorway, she would

The M4, looking east, between junctions 4 and 3.

have more sense than to walk along the carriageway to seek help or an emergency phone! But the hard shoulder was empty – there was no broken-down vehicle to be seen. Shaken she turned off the motorway at the next junction and reported what she had seen to the police. The motorway was searched but no trace of the mysterious woman was found.

A month later, driving with her partner, our witness saw the figure again, at the same location but this time at about six in the evening when the motorway was far busier. She saw the apparition but her partner did not. He did not believe her story but she insisted on coming off the motorway at junction three and returning on the opposite carriageway for another look. This time neither of them saw anything.

Was it possible for someone to walk through such fast-moving traffic and not be hit? Twice within a few weeks? Why was she staring so unflinchingly as the passing cars all but ran her down?

Who was the sad woman in black?

SOMETHING UNEXPECTED IN THE KITCHEN

The church and former stable block in Cranford Park make up an unlikely rural survival so close to Heathrow Airport. St Dunstan's is noteworthy for its remarkable and colourful monuments to members of the Berkeley family, now more closely associated with Gloucestershire.

Cranford House no longer stands but in its day it had a reputation for ghosts, the most famous of which was seen by the Honourable Grantley Berkeley and his younger brother one night in the eighteenth century. The story goes that the two young men had been out chasing foxes one night (an alternative version says they had been on the look out for poachers) and returned to the house in the small hours. Grantley's evocative account was reproduced over a century later by Walter Jerrold in *Highways and Byways of Middlesex*, published in 1909.

'The large old house was as still as death when my hand turned the handle of the kitchen door, which opening, partially admitted me to the room, at the

Cranford House (demolished 1945) and St Dunstan's church.

(Hounslow Cultural and Community Services)

bottom of the long table which, starting from between the entrance where I was and the door to the scullery, ran to my left in its full length to the great fireplace and tall and expansive kitchen screen.

'The screen stood to the right of the fireplace as I looked at it so that a large body of glowing embers in the grate threw a steady distinct glare of red light throughout the entire length of the large apartment making the smallest thing distinctly visible and falling full on the tall figure of a woman, divided from me only by the breadth of the table.

'She was dressed, or seemed to be dressed, as a maidservant, with a sort of poke bonnet on and a dark shawl drawn or pinned tightly across her breast. On my entrance she turned her head to look at me and as she did so every feature ought to have stood forth in the light of the fire – but I at once saw that there was beneath the bonnet an indistinctness of outline not to be accounted for.

'Holding the door open with my left hand with my right against the post, I addressed my brother, who was behind me, simply the word "Look!". As I uttered this, the figure seemed to commence gliding, rather than proceeding by steps, slowly on up the kitchen towards the fireplace, while I lowered my right arm from the post and turned to let my brother in, then closed the door, locked it and put they key into my pocket.'

What the two aristocratic brothers hoped for by locking themselves in the kitchen with the young serving girl it is impossible to speculate. They were out of luck though. They looked everywhere, 'into every nook and corner that could have held a rat' and even up the chimney but the wench was nowhere to be found. It was only later that one of the servants told Grantley that the figure was a ghost and that she had been seen in the kitchen on many previous occasions.

Grantley also told the tale of his father, on a summer evening, seeing a stranger at the top of some cellar steps. No-one should have been there so he challenged him. But the man just disappeared down the steps and no trace of him could be found. However the writer admitted that it was possible that this man was an intruder who, for whatever reason, was protected from discovery by the maidservants.

There seems to have been no such plausible explanation in the case of yet another spirit encountered by Grantley's father. Thinking he had caught a trespasser at the stables, he lashed out at the man with his horsewhip. The whip went straight through the figure, which disappeared.

CREEPY COMPUTERS AT THE RED HOUSE

Journalists are usually too matter-of-fact and sceptical to have much belief in the supernatural – although they never let this fact get in the way of a good story. However the Red House, Cranford, one-time home to the *Hounslow Chronicle* and *Skyport News*, has a somewhat strange reputation. Footsteps heard on the deserted stairway from time to time could be dismissed as the creaking of an old building but many believed there was more to it than that.

The Red House – just to add colour to the story, it is actually painted white – was built by Moreton, the sixth Earl of Berkeley. Preferring the more amiable life

The Red House (now painted white), Cranford.

of a country squire and having no interest in the trappings and responsibilities of bearing a title, he wanted somewhere that could be an escape from the cares of Cranford House, the family home across the park. In particular, he wanted to keep some distance between himself and his eccentric and strong-willed mother. Moreton died in the Red House and his coffin was carried across the park by six of the estate workers to a resting place in the family vault at St Dunstan's church.

Some time after the Second World War it was discovered that the vault had become flooded and an Exhumations Order was granted for his coffin and the remains of other family members to be moved and re-interred in a new vault at the east end of the church. It is said that the sixth Earl objected to being carted around in this undignified manner.

One morning, years later, a member of the editorial staff who had arrived early for work at the Red House was making himself a cup of coffee in the small kitchen when he saw what he thought was a colleague pass by the doorway. Taking his mug with him, he went to have a chat – only to discover that he was still alone in the building.

The same thing happened to the editor of *Skyport News*. He was on the telephone one evening after the rest of the staff had left for home. He thought he heard the door open and someone come in but knew that nobody else should have been there. 'Hang on a minute,' he said, putting the phone aside, and went to investigate. Again, there was nobody there.

Then there was the occasion where a lady editor of the *Chronicle* was alone in the first floor editorial office. She had urgent work to complete. All the computer screens were turned off and she was startled when they suddenly came on, apparently of their own accord. Thinking there was some glitch in the system, she went round turning them off, doubtless muttering about how you could not trust modern technology. After a short while the screens came on again, unnerving the poor woman.

'This is no place to be on my own,' she thought as she hastily turned everything off again, gathered up her belongings and left the building. As she did so, the office doors slammed shut.

She never worked late on her own again. In fact, she left the paper soon afterwards.

THE MESSENGER OF DOOM

Harbingers of doom, death and destruction feature in many tales of the supernatural. One such story comes from the prosaic suburb of Hayes and was vouched for by Mr A.L. Summers in the *Middlesex Quarterly* magazine in 1955. 'The most weird, baffling and dramatic story which created a profound sensation at the time,' he wrote, claiming 'it is perfectly true, the people involved in the drama being well-known to the present writer.'

He described a December evening in 1948 when a visitor staying at a house in a quiet road anxiously asked his hostess if she knew who lived at a particular house at the other end of the road. 'Is the lady big and very tall?' he asked.

He was told that it was more or less the opposite – the lady of that house was rather small. He looked worried and said, 'Then I fear those unfortunate people are in for serious trouble,' explaining that as he was passing their house he saw 'a very tall woman with a halo round her head' hurrying up the garden path to the front door.

Nothing happened for several days, but, soon after the visitor returned home to the north of England, the man of the house where he had seen the apparition was taken seriously ill and taken to hospital, where he died just before Christmas. Within days the wife was also being carried off in an ambulance and she died a few days later.

Had the visitor from the north – who had not known this unfortunate couple – been possessed of psychic or occult powers? Who or what was the 'woman with a halo' that he undoubtedly saw?

Mr Summers does not say but strangely he ended his story with this little poem which seems to suggest that ghostly visitations in the locality were becoming less common:

The ghosts of Hayes are shy these days
And seldom can be seen:
Their visits, which were once a craze,
Now few and far between.

Some careless wraiths have vanished quite,
Just disappeared – like ghosts – one night,
And lost themselves – in haze!

Such a punning little rhyme suggests to me that perhaps Mr Summers did not take the matter terribly seriously.

The Black Raven of St Martin's

Set back in a quiet street, St Martin's church at West Drayton stands near an attractive red brick Tudor gateway, which is all that is left of the ancient manor house that was pulled down in the middle of the eighteenth century. It was built when its owner William Paget was at the height of his power as Secretary of State to Henry VIII. Pride comes before a fall, however, for in the reign of the young Edward VI he was imprisoned in the Tower of London, heavily fined and deprived of many of his honours.

The church today is unusual in that a recent refurbishment turned the interior of the building around so that the altar is at the west rather than the east end. Whether this reordering confused the famous Black Raven that once haunted the church, I do not know. The spectre was reported to be as large as a vulture and 'as black as hell'. It used to be seen flying inside the chancel, down in the vaults and even perched on the Communion rails.

The story goes back to 1749 when strange sounds and knockings were heard coming from the vaults below the church. It was here where the local gentry, the Pagets and De Burghs, were buried but so, it is alleged, were also a murderer and his victim. The murderer, it is said, had committed suicide but being a member of a wealthy and influential family, his shame was hushed up and he was buried in the vault rather than being buried at a crossroads with a stake through his heart, the normal fate of those who had taken their own lives. The infamous raven was his tortured spirit that could never find peace.

Villagers heard a screeching sound coming from the vault and, when they looked through the grating, saw the bird pecking at the coffins. They reported this to the Parish Clerk and were perhaps somewhat disconcerted that this worthy did not seem particularly alarmed for he had seen it himself and so had his wife and daughter. Curiously, it was said to always appear on a Friday.

On another occasion some bellringers saw the Black Raven on the roof. Being brave lads they determined to prove that it was real and not a ghost at all. They threw stones at it and apparently damaged one of its wings. The injured bird was seen to drop down into a corner, shrieking and flapping its wings wildly. Eagerly they rushed to capture their prize but when two of them approached the bird it vanished before their eyes.

In 1883 the wife of a former vicar, not someone likely to repeat spooky tales you would think, said that in the 1850s she had often heard the sound of a big bird flapping its wings, although she had never actually seen it. The raven was seen though in 1869 when two ladies, arranging the altar flowers, saw the bird perched on one of the pews.

What the Black Raven would make of the radically modernised building that is St Martin's today, I shudder to think. But then I dare say the changes came in for some criticism from some of the living parishioners as well!

•Tales from the North-West Frontier•

Northolt Ghosts

Drawing by Hugh Thomson from Highways and Byways of Middlesex (1909).

The thirteenth-century church at Northolt still has the feel of a remote village church and as late as 1908 one writer described the place as 'the most rustic village in Wild West Middlesex' but today it is almost the archetypical suburb.

But even Northolt has its ghosts – in fact, no fewer than four of them, according to an article in the *Middlesex Quarterly* magazine in 1956.

The most famous is that of Sir Nicholas Brembre, Lord of the Manor from 1371 to 1388. He seemed to be a secure member of the fourteenth-century 'great and the good' – he was a favourite of the young King Richard II and was Lord Mayor of London on four occasions. But he must have made some powerful enemies for he was brought to trial for treason before the notorious Merciless Parliament in 1388. The trial was rigged and he was executed with typical medieval brutality at Tyburn.

It is said that on the anniversary of his death he rides round the moat of Northolt Manor, mounted on a white charger, with his head tucked under his arm.

A more serene spectacle, perhaps, is associated with the area near the White Hart at West End. Here, perhaps particularly after closing time, passers-by might be lucky enough to see 'a beautiful lady in a glamorous silk dress'.

Servants at Islips Manor (now the site of a recreation ground) are alleged to have been frightened by a poltergeist who pulled the pillows away while they were asleep and blew in their faces. Mere high-jinks in the attics? Perhaps, but Mr C.H. Keene of the Northolt Local History Society wrote that an old resident assured him that 'some seventy years ago no servant would sleep at the Manor'.

There was also, according to Mr Keene, the story of a ghost being put to rest at Gurneys Farm, Kingshill, when the vicar of the time held a service of exorcism, 'apparently with great success'. Kingshill Avenue and Gurneys Road, Yeading, are all that is left of this tale today, I fear.

There could even have been more ghostly goings-on. Two pagan Saxon burials were found in the 1950s under the kitchens at Northolt Manor. One grave contained a female skeleton but the second one had been disturbed in medieval times and used as a rubbish pit. Any self-respecting spirit might have been expected to protest at such treatment by doing a bit of haunting!

ALONG THE ARTERIAL ROAD

Motorists struggling along the A40 arterial road towards London might be forgiven if the spirit world does not enter too much into their consciousness. Those who have travelled this road over many years might, though, have time to reflect on how much the district has changed over time.

How much more disconcerting the twentieth-century developments must have been to the ghosts and spirits that lurk in what was a quiet rural backwater a hundred years ago. Nora Robinson, in an article published in the *Middlesex Quarterly* in 1956 tells the story of several of them.

'I thought it was someone looking for a job till I noticed his clothes,' said a workman on an Alperton factory site in 1930. It seems that it was only when the figure suddenly vanished into thin air that the workman realised that he had seen a ghost.

The Coston family memorial in Holy Cross church at Greenford.

It was then discovered that a certain Tom Bowler had been executed for attempted murder on the same spot in 1812 and his ghost had allegedly been seen many times after that. 'Was the apparition interested in the new factory going up on his favourite hunting-ground,' asks Nora Robinson, 'or had he absent-mindedly forgotten the fact and imagined that he was still haunting the former country lanes he remembered?'

A noted philanthropist and benefactor to the community in his day, Simon Coston died in 1666. The family memorial can be seen in the ancient parish church of Holy Cross at Greenford – a gem of a building that stands incongruously adjacent to a larger church begun in 1939. The new church was built in response to the rapid inter-war growth in population as the ribbon development stretched out from London along the arterial road.

This suburban expansion disturbed the ghost of old Simon who had, it seems, been cheerfully haunting the scenes of his earthly life for almost three hundred years. As Nora Robinson put it, he could not see 'why he shouldn't continue to do so, housing estates notwithstanding!'. She claims that 'he was last reported to be walking around aimlessly, apparently looking over a half-completed council house with all mod cons'.

Simon Coston's wealth is alleged to have been acquired when, as a young boy, he dared to enter the lair of the famous old miser of Perivale Windmill. The miser's ghost is reported to have been seen between the wars, still counting his coins by an eerie flickering light.

He too was disturbed by the new world of the 1930s. 'When Perivale became a modern industrial district,' Nora wrote, 'he seems to have decided it was time to take himself and his coins elsewhere – otherwise he would probably have been mistaken for just another wages clerk by the factory staff!'

DIRTY DEEDS AT BLACK JACK'S LOCK

The pleasant walk along the Grand Union Canal towpath from Uxbridge north towards Rickmansworth brings you to Black Jack's Lock, near Harefield. It seems peaceful enough now but in the days when working boats travelled the canals, superstitious boatmen would not moor overnight there.

Apparently a landowner in the canal's early days around 1800 employed a negro named Black Jack to harrass the boatmen whom he did not want anywhere near his land. Black Jack did his job well and was so disliked by the boatmen that he was murdered after he had dangerously interfered with locks and stolen their windlasses.

But Black Jack came back to haunt them and the tale of his ghostly appearances spread the length of the Grand Union and beyond, so that no crew passed the spot without a fearful shudder.

The canal historian Hugh McKnight could write as late as 1975, 'No doubt there is more than an element of truth in the legend.'

The canal around Regent's Park, near London Zoo, is haunted by the crew of *Tilbury*, one of three barges loaded with gunpowder, which blew up in

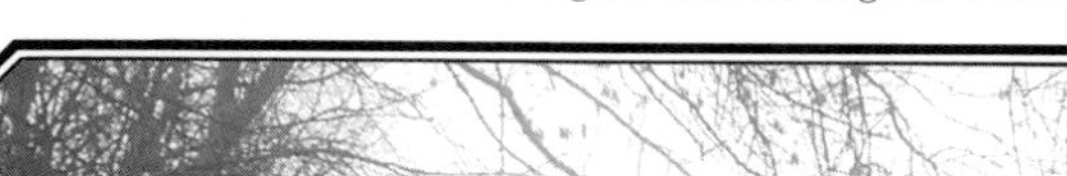

Islington Tunnel, Regents Canal

October 1874 killing all three of them and demolishing a bridge. More tangible evidence of this tragedy is that when the bridge (known as Macclesfield Bridge) was rebuilt, the iron columns salvaged from the wreckage were put back facing the wrong way, so that the abrasions caused by towropes rubbing on the metal over the years are now in a position where no ropes could ever have cut them.

A little way further along the canal, beyond the wastelands of King's Cross and St Pancras, is Islington Tunnel. Several canal tunnels claim the ghost of Kit Crewbucket, a murdered woman whose body was disposed of in their murky waters. Many old boaters claim to have seen her spectre – but she seems to have put herself about a bit because similar tales are associated with canal tunnels in other parts of the country!

The Warrior of Horsenden Hill

The canal still winds around the foot of Horsenden Hill at Perivale, an attractive rural oasis north of the industrial sprawl along Western Avenue. Romantic legend says that the hill is so called after Horsa, a famous Anglo-Saxon chieftain, whose wife enjoyed nightly revels and partying with the fairy folk in the valley below – earning it the name of 'Fairyvale', which over time became Perivale.

Stern academic experts in place names may disagree, I fear.

She gave birth to their only child, Ealine, a beautiful girl who soon outstripped what her mother could teach her and became something of a child prodigy. She fell in love with and married Bren, the handsome chief of a powerful tribe based on the north bank of the Thames – appropriately enough at Brentford!

Sadly Ealine did not live happily ever after. Rather than indulge in erudite conversations with his intellectual young wife, Bren preferred boozing and carousing with the lads. If they had had counsellors in those days they would have diagnosed a dysfunctional marriage but clever Ealine had the measure of her erring husband. She trained a starling to speak – not something Bren

The view from Horsenden Hill.

would have thought of – and sent it winging over the fields to Horsenden Hill to tell her father how badly she was being treated.

Horsa and his band of warriors sallied forth to the ford that bore Bren's name and a mighty battle ensued. Bren was killed outright and Horsa mortally wounded but Ealine came home in righteous triumph to attend her father's funeral.

He was buried on Horsenden Hill alongside his favourite horse. Local folk do say that Horsa's giant steed can be heard pacing about his tomb and the shadowy form of the great warrior is seen 'on nights when the pale moon illuminates the hill and white mists curl upwards from the vale at its foot'.

THE BOY IN THE BOX

The seventeenth-century mansion of Swakeleys at Ickenham is associated with a number of tales which, if not exactly ghost stories, are distinctly macabre. Owning this magnificent pile does not seem to have brought its owners much luck – indeed, at times it must have seemed as if the place was cursed. The house was completed in 1638 for Sir Edmund Wright, a member of the prestigious Grocers' Company, who became an alderman and lord mayor of London. He was not able to enjoy its splendours for very long, for he died in 1643.

Under his will it passed to his daughter Catherine, the wife of Sir James Harrington, with the slightly curious provision that she should entertain her relatives there for a fortnight each year. Sir James was a noted Parliamentarian at the time of the Civil War and was a judge in the subsequent trial which condemned Charles I to death. He was therefore obliged to flee the country when the monarchy was restored in 1660. Catherine stayed on for a while but the house was put up for sale within a few years.

Sir Robert Clayton, described by his friend the historian Macauley as 'the wealthiest merchant in London, was keen to buy Swakeleys, and it was there on 16th August 1665 that his wife Mary gave birth to their only son. Sadly the baby died the same day and there is a poignant monument to him in St Giles' church, Ickenham, with a carved stone effigy of the child. Even this sad relic had an unlucky history. At some time in the past it was discarded and lost until it was dug up from the churchyard in 1921. It is now next to a window in the chancel.

In view of its unhappy associations, it was no surprise that Sir Robert decided not to purchase the property and Swakeleys was instead purchased by a wealthy goldsmith, Sir Robert Vyner. Samuel Pepys visited Sir Robert there in order to borrow money on behalf of the impoverished Charles II. His diary records that his host kept a curious and rather repellent relic in the house: 'a black boy he had, that died of consumption, and being dead he caused him to be dried in an oven, and lies entire there in a box.' It was, to say the least, a gruesome taste in curios.

After Sir Robert died in 1688 the house had various owners until it was purchased in 1750 by Reverend Thomas Clarke, rector of Ickenham. He must have known about the ill-fortune which had dogged successive owners but he seemed untroubled by it – and rightly so, for his family remained in possession until 1922.

Even so, there are still two more untimely deaths to record. In 1776 Swakeleys was inherited by Thomas Truesdale Clarke, the eldest son of Reverend Thomas's second marriage. He was an influential man locally, a magistrate, who successfully built up the estate and lived well. Yet he died a strange death at the age of 66 in 1840. He was found dead in the River Pinn where it ran through his park. He was lying on his back in less than two feet of water which barely covered his face. His body was out of the water and dry.

It was said that he had been depressed for some time but the inquest jury declined to bring in a verdict of suicide as there was no evidence to support this. The coroner stated that he thought 'it would be best not to stamp the family of the deceased with the stigma of insanity'.

While the inquest was taking place at the Coach & Horses at Ickenham, Mrs Clarke's groom, James Winch, hanged himself in an outhouse at his cottage in the village. His family was not afforded the same consideration, the verdict being that he had 'committed suicide while suffering temporary insanity'. Perhaps the word 'temporary' was inserted to suggest that it was really only a short-term problem and nothing to worry about!

Subsequent occupants of Swakeleys seem to have had more tranquil lives. Mr Clarke's son, another Thomas, was described in his obituary as 'the life and soul of many a merry party during the shooting season' and staged amateur theatricals every February. In the 1890s Swakeleys was leased by Arthur Gilbey of the gin distilling family. He was a devotee of croquet and the All England Croquet Championship was played on Swakeleys' lawns. The curse – if there ever was one – seems to have been lifted.

•Spooks in the Suburbs•

The Phantom Number 7 Bus

A present-day Number 7 bus

It always used to be said that London Buses were either never there when you wanted one or else they came along in threes. The patient queues waiting in the rain on a cold evening might sometimes have wondered whether their bus had disappeared into some mysterious black hole on the way from the depot! Certainly one of the strangest of stories concerns the phantom Number 7 bus in North Kensington.

A red London bus has several times appeared in spectral form at the junction of St Mark's Road and Cambridge Gardens. It appears on a blind corner speeding down the road in the small hours and has been the cause of a number of accidents.

One witness told investigators: 'I was turning the corner and saw a bus tearing towards me. The lights of the top and bottom decks and the headlights were full on but I could see no sign of the crew or passengers. I yanked my steering wheel hard over and mounted the pavement, scraping the roadside wall. The bus just vanished.'

In another crash, in June 1934, a driver was killed when his car swerved off the road for no apparent reason, hit a lamp-post and burst into flames. At the inquest an eyewitness said that he had seen a bus hurtling towards the car just before it left the road. The coroner queried this but other local residents confirmed to him and to the media that they too had seen the phantom bus. One, who worked at the bus garage, even claimed that it had drawn into the bus depot, stood with its engine running and then disappeared.

The story was always the same. Witnesses agreed that it was a number 7 bus in the colours of the London General Omnibus Company. The LGOC became the London Passenger Transport Board in 1933 after which all buses had 'London Transport' on the side, rather than 'General' as the phantom bus did. Incidents involving the bus always seemed to happen at about 1.15 a.m., which was an unlikely time for a Number 7 to be about.

Eventually the road junction was remodelled, eliminating the blind spot. This piece of municipal exorcism seems to have done the trick and the phantom bus is seen no more. My photograph, taken in 2003, shows a more modern Routemaster bus (presumably a real one).

Has the Wind Changed?

Kensington, now very much part of London, was a village in rural Middlesex in the seventeenth and eighteenth centuries. Kensington Palace, which is still one of its showpiece glories, was reconstructed by Sir Christopher Wren for William and Mary and remodelled again by William Kent for King George I.

Kensington Palace.

It is George II whose ghost is alleged to haunt the palace. During his last days the old King was very ill, confined to his apartments at Kensington and awaiting news of his ships coming from the continent. The country was at war and things were not going well. The fleet was prevented from sailing by contrary winds and the King was watching the weathervane anxiously.

For George the good news never did come. He died before the wind veered. Several witnesses report seeing the ghost of the King looking out of the window and even hearing the question, in his thick German accent, 'Has the wind changed?'

Another ghost alleged to haunt the Palace is Princess Sophia, daughter of George III. In what was a great royal scandal in its day, the young Princess slept with Thomas Garth, one of the King's equerries. The inevitable happened and she had a baby boy – imagine what today's tabloid newspapers would make of such an event! Thomas seems to have been something of a bad lot because he paid little attention to poor Sophia after the child was born and she lived out a sad and lonely life at Kensington. She spent a lot of time at her spinning wheel but as she grew old and blind even this solace was denied her. It is said that a phantom spinning wheel has been seen in her old room at the palace and its creaking sound has been heard on a number of occasions.

Nearby Holland House was designed in Stuart times by John Thorpe for Sir William Rich, Earl of Holland. It was a house of great splendour with oriel windows, Dutch gables and a stone balustrade. During the Civil War it was for a time the headquarters of the Parliamentary Army.

In days long gone the headless ghost of the Earl of Holland was seen wandering through the Gilt Room. Sadly most of the house was destroyed by bombing during 1940. Part of the East Wing survived and it later became a Youth Hostel. The headless Earl seems to have survived the wartime destruction. He has often been seen in the Gilt Room, holding his head in both hands as he appears from a hidden doorway at midnight and walking slowly around the room. Three spots of blood are said to mark the place where he appears – and these spots just cannot be removed! Occasionally the ghost decides to pop out for a breath of air. He was seen in the garden by some students in 1965.

Legend has it that all three of Rich's daughters, Lady Diana, Lady Isabella and Lady Mary had premonitions of their untimely deaths, seeing their ghostly faces in a mirror shortly beforehand.

A phantom fried breakfast is a mouthwatering but tantalising prospect but this is what researcher Andrew Green claims to have come across at Chiswick House. One afternoon in the early 1970s he was visiting the house, which was designed by the Earl of Burlington in 1725. The building was being restored at the time so there were a lot of workmen on site. Mr Green became aware of 'a strong and unmistakable smell of frying eggs and bacon'. He remarked to the foreman that someone must be enjoying a very late breakfast. The foreman laughed and said, 'It's the ghost of one of the mad cooks!'

Apparently the appetising smell had been noticed by several people over the years. Mr Green was told by Michael Digby, Head Custodian at the time and a former Mayor of Brentford and Chiswick, that the phenomenon was experienced at irregular intervals – sometimes for two days in a row and then

Chiswick House.

nothing for several months. The smell is only apparent in the north wing, where the kitchens used to be until they were demolished over a century ago.

A teacher in charge of a group of schoolchildren visiting Osterley Park House near Isleworth was puzzled when three of her pupils asked 'Who is the lovely lady in the white dress?' Several other children had also seen this mysterious woman in a flowing gown, moving towards the entrance from an archway under the main staircase. One of the attendants said that he had heard stories before of 'the White Lady of Osterley' and Andrew Green met two workers who had seen her during renovations. She was a creature of habit, it seems, usually appearing at half past four in the afternoon. Perhaps she was wondering what had happened to tea!

Peculiar Feelings in Ealing

A featureless modern block of flats at 16 Montpelier Road, Ealing now stands on the site where there was formerly a Victorian house with a sinister reputation for encouraging suicides. Its grisly history was told by Andrew Green in his 1975 book, *Our Haunted Kingdom.*

The evils began in 1887 when a twelve-year-old girl called Anne Hinchfield threw herself to her death from the top of the seventy-foot tower that was a feature of this sinister property. In 1934 Mr Green's mother, a nurse, was called to the house – a nursemaid had thrown her charge from the same tower and then jumped after her to her death. The police doctor was examining the bodies

16 Montpelier Road, Ealing.
(Sketch by the author)

Flats on the site of the ill-omened 16 Montpelier Road, Ealing.

and Mrs Green waited in the back garden. She saw footsteps mysteriously appear on the wet grass in front of her. These footprints stopped at a garden seat, which moved slightly, as if someone had sat down on it.

The house was said to have an evil atmosphere and a strange smell emanating every four weeks. A malevolent spirit, it is believed, somehow convinced the 'suicides' that they were stepping out into the garden, rather than from the top of the tower. Visitors reported feeling strange hands assisting them climbing the tower stairs and an almost irresistible urge to jump from the top.

In all twenty suicides and the murder of the child are believed to have taken place from the tower at 16 Montpelier Road. After the 1934 tragedy the house stood empty for more than ten years.

In 1944 the intrepid Mr Green visited it with his father. In *Our Haunted Kingdom* he speaks of unseen hands helping him up the ladder to the top of the tower. He felt impelled to look down into the garden. It was as if a voice was saying to him, 'Walk over the parapet, it's only twelve inches to the lawn. You won't hurt yourself.'

At that moment his father, who perhaps ought to have been alert to the possibility of something awful happening to his son, grabbed him by the scruff of the neck, preventing another so-called 'suicide'.

After the war the house was converted into flats but odd things kept on happening, including gas leaks which could not be traced by gas board engineers. In 1970 the present block of flats replaced the sinister old house but even now the residents are troubled by mysterious noises.

Visitor at Midnight

Writing in 1871 Augustus Hare recalled a curious happening at Harrow School some time before. It seems that a gentleman by the name of Mr Merivale had been staying as a guest at the school but was unexpectedly summoned back to London late at night.

As his horsedrawn fly conveyed him away from the school at midnight, both Merivale and a friend travelling with him were surprised to see a Hackney cab outside the headmaster's house. It was a most unlikely time for the headmaster to be receiving visitors. Even more curious was the figure of a man in black that they both saw get down from the cab and glide into the house, apparently without ringing the bell or the door being opened. On their journey towards London they both agreed that this was indeed what they had seen and that it was mysterious and inexplicable.

When Mr Merivale returned to Harrow the next day he called at the house and asked whether the headmaster, Dr Butler, was at home. The servant who greeted him said that he was not.

'Who then was the strange gentleman who visited him at midnight?' Mr Merivale asked.

The servant replied that there had been no visitor and no Hackney cab but at that exact hour and in a distant part of the country the headmaster's father had died.

Headmaster's House, Harrow School.

HENDON HAUNTINGS

The churchyard of the parish church at Hendon played a curious part in the creation of Bram Stoker's classic story, *Dracula*.

In 1892 when he was writing the novel, Stoker was manager of the Lyceum Theatre and doubtless would have seen the enthusiastic review of Henry Irving's production of *King Lear* published in the influential *Lloyd's Weekly Newspaper*. His eye might well have fallen on a report on the opposite page concerning certain macabre events at Hendon, a place he knew well as he had friends there.

The story concerned a young man who, in 1828, petitioned the vicar to allow the family vault to be opened. He had urgent and pressing reasons to do so, he said. The vicar reluctantly gave permission on the understanding that the coffins remained unopened. He must have been horror-stricken when the young man, who was clearly deranged, was caught hacking off the head of his mother who had died nineteen years previously. Apparently he was a medical student obsessed with the idea that he was dying from the hereditary disease which had killed her.

Nearby, to the east of the church was the sinister-looking Rundell mausoleum. Scholars believe that this structure fits Stoker's description of the tomb occupied by his heroine – 'a lordly death-house in a lonely churchyard away from teeming London'. Hendon was indeed still a remote rural community then. They go on to claim that when Bram Stoker described how Van Elsing severed poor Lucy Westenra's head from her body in order to bring her soul to rest he was remembering those strange events at Hendon more than sixty years before.

The Kingsbury Green and Hyde areas at Colindale, which is next to Hendon, were plagued by the ghost of a haymaker who had quarrelled with another farmworker and been stabbed to death with a pitchfork. It was a particularly aggressive phantom, keen to inflict a similar fate on those unfortunate enough to cross his path. An even more bizarre apparition in Hyde Lane is the ghostly and polychromatic donkey, alleged to dazzle the beholder with its coat of many colours! In Colindeep Lane the spirit of the ill-used Mrs Griffiths appears. She drowned herself in a pond when allegedly 'maddened by drink'.

Colindeep Lane is quite a thoroughfare for the departed, it seems. J.A. Brooks in *Ghosts of London* (1982) quotes an account by nineteenth century folklorist, J.P. Emslie, of another ghost seen walking towards Hendon. A policeman apparently 'saw a man a little in front of him and walked faster to catch him up for the sake of having his company. Not catching the man, he went on increasing his speed until he was running hard, and yet could never catch the man, who suddenly disappeared. The policeman was so frightened that his hair stood up on end to such an extent that it lifted his hat off his head and a few days afterwards he died of fright.'

J.P. Emslie took a particular interest in local ghost stories, collecting them between 1860 and 1893. The notebooks were edited by F. Celoria for the first issue of the journal *London Studies* in 1974. Another of his tales concerns Honeypot Lane in Stanmore. The twentieth century saw it become an

Colindeep Lane, Hendon.

industrial estate, a far cry from the scene of a battle said to have taken place there when the Romans, led by Julius Caesar invaded Britain. A great rushing sound is heard there on dark nights and witnesses speak of 'something horrible' brushing past them.

The RAF museum at Hendon is home to a magnificent collection of historic aircraft, including Spitfires, Mosquitos, Lancasters and the last surviving Wellington bomber.

It is hardly surprising that these planes, which must have taken part in so many scenes of death and destruction, sometimes stir remembrances of things past. Witnesses, including former directors of the museum, are unable to explain the various odd noises, bumps and bangings, footsteps, the sound of engine cowlings being lifted and the distinctive throbbing sound of aircraft engines idling that are sometimes heard by staff in the hangars late at night.

At the RAF museum, Colindale near Hendon.

Some say that these disturbances go back to the death of Flight Lieutenant Shepherd, killed when his training aircraft crashed in 1917 – but this would surely not account for the manifestations affecting the Second World War aircraft!

There is an Armed Services connection also to the story of the Three Crowns pub in Nan Clarke's Lane at nearby Mill Hill. There is a legend that the unfortunate Miss Clarke was a barmaid who was murdered. According to an article in an issue of the *Middlesex Quarterly* published in 1954, she can occasionally be seen walking along the lane, 'carrying her head in her hand'. Some soldiers of the Middlesex Regiment, stationed nearby during the Second World War, 'declared that they saw this apparition', although at what stage in their evening's drinking is not recorded! Do not go there to check for youself as I did on a very warm day. After puffing all the way up from Mill Hill I discovered that the Three Crowns is long gone and there is now no pub in Nan Clarke's Lane!

Not far away at West Finchley, Nether Street was the scene in the nineteenth-century of appearances of a mysterious 'White Lady'. Local legend has it that one policeman sent to investigate the sightings became so obsessed with the ghost after seeing it that he ended his days in a lunatic asylum.

During the Second World War an upstairs room in the council offices at Avenue House, East End Road in Finchley was converted into a dormitory for the women who were operating the switchboard. However, a ghost regularly disturbed the girls, always approaching one particular bed – regardless of which young lady was occupying it – having entered the room without opening the door. After a little while it would leave the room the same way.

At least, one hopes it was a ghost!

MONKS, NUNS AND A DEAD BEATLE

St Mary's church at Neasden is a Victorian building but parts remain from the original medieval structure. It is said to be haunted by the ghost of a priest, accompanied by the smell of incense. He also makes his presence known by rattling door handles in the vestry. The well-fed figure of a rotund monk in a black habit has been seen near the vicarage. He is a very non-threatening fellow, happy-looking and taking pleasure in the garden.

There are more spectral monks – lots of them – at St Dunstan's church in East Acton, a site that had monastic connections in the Middle Ages. Up to a dozen have been seen walking in procession up the central aisle to the accompaniment of beautiful music. They are said to appear every four years.

Peter Underwood, President of the Ghost Club and a member of the Society for Psychical Research, visited the church and spoke to the vicar at the time, the Reverend Hugh Anton-Stevens, who confirmed the story. A former naval lieutenant backed him up and said that he had purposely stood in the path of the line of hooded figures but they had passed right through him and he had felt nothing. Mr Underwood himself, perhaps to his disappointment, did not observe anything odd while he was there. At Edmonton several people have seen a phantom white dog in the churchyard but, so long as you ignore

St Dunstan's church, East Acton.

it, they say it is quite harmless.

Old Church Farm at Stanmore was formerly the rectory and is haunted by the ghost of a parson. He has been seen to rise from his grave opposite the house, walk towards it and then return. He seems to be another kindly soul, particularly concerned if there is someone in the house who is ill. Odd noises and knocking on walls accompany his visits.

Reverend John Smyth-Pigott once lived at 12 Langford Place, St John's Wood. He was an Anglican clergyman who in the 1890s announced to the world that he was actually Jesus Christ. His congregation in Clapton seemed to be convinced by his claim. He called his church 'The Ark of the Covenant' but preferred to live out in leafy St John's Wood in an architectural fantasy house called 'The Agapemone', the Abode of Love. It was said that some of the more comely of his female acolytes were summoned there to become 'Brides of Christ'. After his death Smyth-Pigott was buried beneath a marble slab in his church, his body standing upright so as to be ready for his resurrection.

Sir John Betjeman visited The Agapemone when making his classic television film *Metroland* in 1973. 'Did they strew their Lord with lilies?' he asked rhetorically, 'I don't know – but for some reason this house has an uncanny atmosphere, threatening and restless. Someone seems to be looking over your shoulder.'

Abbey Road zebra crossing, St John's Wood. The EMI recording studios are on the left.

Langford Place is a turning off Abbey Road, close to the EMI studios where the Beatles made their recordings in the 1960s. The cover of the LP that bears the studios' name became the centre of a bizarre and widely-circulated myth that the Paul McCartney figure seen on the zebra crossing was in fact a 'ghost'! It was said that Paul had been killed in a car crash in November 1966 and that the Beatles had, for financial reasons, decided to keep his death a secret.

George Tremlett in *The Paul McCartney Story* (1975) described how great play was made of the fact that Ringo Starr appeared to be dressed as an undertaker, George Harrison as a gravedigger and John Lennon as a clergyman. Paul appeared walking barefoot – and in Italy bare feet traditionally symbolised a corpse! Some even noted that the parked Volkswagen pictured on the LP sleeve had the numberplate 281 F, taken to mean that McCartney would have been 28 IF he had lived.

Other pieces of 'evidence' to support this claim were the letters OPD appearing on an armband in another sleeve photo of Paul, the letters standing for 'Officially Pronounced Dead', and the fact that in another photo he was seen to be wearing a black flower when the other three Beatles all had red ones.

It was all nearly forty years ago but the crossing is still something of a place of pilgrimage. When I was there in February 2004 there were groups of Japanese teenagers taking photographs of each other and the street sign and walls of Abbey Road were decorated with recent graffiti proclaiming the fans' undying devotion to the Beatles. Beatlemania was not dead – neither, of course, was Paul McCartney!

In 1963, workmen digging in the grounds of St Joseph's Nursing College in Mill Hill discovered the coffin of a nineteenth-century nun. Shortly afterwards there were several sightings of a cloaked figure in the road nearby. When approached she always disappeared. Curiously, similar appearances had taken place in the 1920s. A phantom nun has also been seen at Amerhurst Lodge in Ealing, a building that was once an orphanage run by nuns. One witness saw her bending over a patient, only to vanish.

A particularly sad story comes from the Central Middlesex Hospital at Park Royal. The building is said to be disturbed by the ghost of a young girl who died there long ago. She had been admitted for what was expected to be a minor operation but tragically was given the wrong anaesthetic and died in the operating theatre. She is not seen there but in the ward where she had been beforehand. Strange clunking noises are heard and the lift to the surgical ward is said to move up and down of its own volition.

Doctor Crippen's Parcel

Hilldrop Crescent, Kentish Town, found unwelcome fame in 1910 as the address of the infamous wife-killer, Dr Hawley Harvey Crippen. It caused a great sensation at the time, not just for the savage nature of the crime, but more particularly because of the unprecedented circumstances of Crippen's arrest. He was apprehended with his mistress on a transatlantic liner, the authorities having been alerted via the newfangled wireless. They must have felt themselves safe as the great ship steamed away from England.

It was later revealed that before the murder, Crippen was frequently seen by residents of Kentish Town wandering late at night around a piece of waste ground near his home. It was assumed that he must have been planning the foul deed or steeling himself to carry it out.

On the night before Crippen's execution, as he lay in his cell contemplating the hangman's noose, someone was watching the waste ground by Hilldrop Crescent. He was startled to see a shadowy figure coming from the direction of the Crippens' house and carrying an oddly-shaped parcel. The figure was heading for a stagnant rubbish-filled pond nearby. A few minutes later the watcher saw the shadow return. It was no longer carrying the parcel! It is said that Mrs Crippen's head and some other parts of her anatomy were never found.

Those with a macabre fascination to see such places for themselves will be disappointed to know that 39 Hilldrop Crescent was demolished many years ago. Breaking a row of identical tall Victorian houses, the site is now occupied by a block of 1930s flats named, Margaret Bondfield House.

Another Kentish Town ghost story comes from more recent times – it was published in the *St Pancras Chronicle* in 1980 – but takes us back much further into history.

A local antique dealer obtained a Spanish suit of armour from a house clearance sale in Hackney. It needed some work to bring it back into good condition but once this was done he placed it in the window of his shop in Grafton Road. Some time later an Arab gentleman parked his Rolls Royce outside and bought the armour, paying the hefty price demanded without any attempt to get a reduction.

Shortly afterwards the hauntings began! There were sightings of a tall, bearded and noble-looking figure, distinguished despite the fact that he was clad only in scanty undergarments of curious design. It seemed obvious that

Margaret Bondfield House, built on the site of 39 Hilldrop Crescent, the home of Dr Crippen.

this was the original owner of the armour, distressed in some way by the fact that it had been sold without his knowledge.

The shop-owner made urgent attempts to trace the mysterious customer but he learned that the suit of armour had already been shipped to the Middle East so the knight was condemned to continue to wander unclad through that antique shop in Kentish Town.

Islington Incredibles

Richard Cloudesley, who died in 1517, was a member of a notable family that had been great benefactors to the parish of Islington. There appeared to be nothing in his life to suggest that he would cause any trouble in death and he was laid to rest at St Mary's church.

However, according to a floridly-written romantic account published by Muggins & Co. of Clerkenwell in 1842, in the area around Cloudesley's grave 'there did take place a wondrous commotion, the earth swelling and turning up on every side, his body being restless on the score of some sin by him peradventure committed, did show or seem to signify that religious observance should there take place to quiet his departed spirit'.

The writer goes on to describe how exorcists working at the grave by torchlight managed eventually 'to set at rest the unruly spirit of the said Richard Cloudesley and the earth did return to its pristine shape, nevermore commotion preceeding therefrom to this day'. It was said that the ghost was only laid after a thousand Masses were said for his soul!

In 1813 his remains were moved to a new location, apparently without any dire consequences. Richard Cloudesley was commemorated in stained glass in Trinity Church, Cloudesley Square, latterly the Pentecostal Celestial Church of Christ.

The Old Queen's Head Inn in Essex Road is a hostelry whose original licence was said to have been granted by Sir Walter Raleigh. Legend has it that Queen Elizabeth I herself had a tunnel constructed from the inn to Canonbury Tower so she could discreetly visit her lover, the Earl of Essex, there.

The old inn was an impressive half-timbered and jettied structure, overhanging the roadway. Strange stories were told of it. One of its upper rooms was sealed off after child plague victims died there in 1665.

This historic building was pulled down in 1829 but landlords of the replacement pub on the site have also been troubled by ghostly visitations, including an Elizabethan lady and a sad-looking little girl. It is said that on the first Sunday of every month doors mysteriously open and close and footsteps are heard on the stairs. Some have heard the sound of a woman's footsteps accompanied by the rustle of a full-skirted dress.

Perhaps this is the Virgin Queen hastening to her lover!

At 113 Bride Street, near Pentonville Prison, latterly the site of a telephone exchange, there was once a chapel of the nonconformist Sandemanian sect.

The rebuilt Old Queens Head, Islington.

Michael Faraday, the scientist, was an Elder of this group and his ghost has apparently been seen there.

A more recent worthy in a very different field of endeavour was the Music Hall impresario, Sam Collins. His theatre stood on Islington Green and apparently he always occupied the same seat (Row B, Seat 6) to check on his artistes. It is said that he continued to do so after his death and that the appearances of his ghost became so familiar that the cleaning women worked around him!

In 1960, becoming restless perhaps, he was seen to walk through the wall of the cellar. It was time to move on in any case as shortly afterwards the old music hall was pulled down.

•Ham and High Jinx•

Drinking Companions

Go out for a quiet drink in Hampstead or Highgate and you may find yourself with some unexpected drinking companions. The historic pubs in this part of north London seem to have more than their fair share of ghostly visitations.

The Spaniards Inn, Hampstead Heath.

Take the Holly Bush Inn on Holly Mount, for example. The pub, built in 1643, is on the site of old stables that went with the nearby house once owned by the painter, George Romney. Its sign recalls the tradition of hanging a green branch or bush to advertise that the house was licensed to sell ale. If, when you sit down at your table in the dining area, a pretty waitress comes to take your order, you may be in for a very long wait. The pub operates an order-at-the-bar system and the girl is one of the two ghosts that frequent this establishment. The other is an unseen hand that is said to pat the pub's pianist on the back when he finishes playing, as if to congratulate him on his performance.

Perhaps the best-known of all Hampstead's inns is the Spaniards on the edge of the Heath. Dick Turpin's father was once landlord there – some say Dick himself was born there – and the ghost of the famous highwayman is alleged to gallop towards the unwary late at night and swerve away at the last minute. Others have heard ghostly hoofbeats in the vicinity of the pub. You would have a job to hear them during the day though because of the constant flow of traffic along Spaniards Road, constricted here by the historic tollhouse opposite. The Spaniards makes much of its Turpin connection and contains a collection of memorabilia relating to him.

At the William IV inn the figure of a girl in a white shroud is seen looking sadly out of a window. It is said that she committed suicide in the dentist's surgery opposite – though whether this was before or after treatment is not recorded! A second female apparition haunts the William IV. She is believed to be a former resident of the building before it was a pub. The story goes that she was murdered by her husband and bricked up in the walls, which should make the management think twice before embarking on any structural alterations. She makes noises, rattles windows and slams doors in the middle of the night in justifiable protest at the treatment she received in life.

The Flask Tavern in Flask Walk, close to Hampstead tube station, has a conservative sort of ghost who does not like change. Monty, believed to be a nineteenth century landlord, makes his feelings felt by moving tables and messing around with the lights if any alterations are made to the interior.

Confusingly there is another haunted pub called the Flask, this time in West Hill, Highgate. Here the ghost is female but no one is quite sure who she is. Some say she is a girl who committed suicide after an unhappy love affair and some that she is the ghost of the sultry-looking beauty portrayed in the picture that hangs in the bar. Or is she somehow linked to the bullet embedded in the wall? She, too, switches lights on and off, moves glasses and there are sudden inexplicable drops in temperature. Some customers have felt something blowing on their necks and when they turn round there is no one there. Richard Jones in *Walking Haunted London* records how a clairvoyant took three friends for lunch at the Flask but the 'overwhelming and disturbing' aura of the ghost meant that they left almost immediately.

The name Highgate derives from the tollgate where travellers, including cattle drovers on their way to Smithfield, had to stop and pay for the privilege of crossing land owned by the Bishop of London. Although rebuilt in 1905, the Gatehouse Inn, recalls this tradition. Before the London Government Act of 1963, the pub lay half in Hornsey, Middlesex, and half in the borough of

St Pancras in London. The boundary markers are still displayed on the outside wall. In the old days the Middlesex Sessions were held at the inn. The old courtroom was on the second floor and the London side of the room was roped off to make sure that the prisoners did not escape into another authority's area with all the complications that would ensue.

The pub is said to be haunted by Mother Marnes, an old lady murdered (along with her cat) for her money inside the old Gatehouse long ago. Considerately, she only comes when there are no children or animals at the pub but, when she does put in an appearance, the black-robed figure's manifestations are said to be terrifying. One landlord apparently was so traumatised by what he saw that he ended up in hospital. The upstairs part of the building, where the ghost appeared, is now an intimate theatre, one of London's most successful 'fringe' venues.

Another theatrical venue with a sinister past is the Mountview Arts Centre at Crouch Hill. The ghost of a little girl dressed in a late Victorian pinafore smock was seen on a number of occasions in the 1970s – once during a rehearsal of *The Importance of Being Earnest*. One member of the theatre staff dismissed his colleagues' sightings of her as 'sheer rubbish' until the night when he felt her take his hand and lead him across the darkened stage. The girl is believed to have been either the victim or perhaps even the perpetrator of a murder which took place in the 1890s in the old school building which now forms the arts centre.

The eighteenth-century houses of Church Row, Hampstead, had a reputation for hauntings back in the 1880s. At one particular property the new owners were soon troubled by the usual manifestations – sounds of footsteps at dead of night, locked doors flying open, a feeling of being watched, or even being touched by invisible fingers. One November afternoon, the lady of the house was reading aloud to her young daughter when she became aware of footsteps, the sounds of furniture being moved about and door handles being turned. She knew that they were alone in the house and felt she wanted to scream but, not wanting to alarm the child who seemed engrossed in the story, she handed the book to her daughter, opened the door and looked around. The sounds ceased and she saw nobody there.

The Gatehouse pub, Highgate.

Yet, when she went back to continue reading, her daughter pointed to the window seat on which the lamplight shone brightest and asked, 'Who is that pretty lady?'

The same house was later alleged to be haunted at first light by the sinister figure of a red-haired serving-maid creeping out carrying a carpet-bag. It was said that she had murdered a child in her care, dismembered its body and sneaked out at dawn with its remains in the bag. Long shuddering sighs were heard, especially in September.

THE FIRST FROZEN CHICKEN

Sir Francis Bacon, Lord Chancellor and Viscount St Albans, was being driven in his coach through Pond Square at Highgate one snowy morning in March 1626. His mind was preoccupied with many matters

– a man of many parts he was, among other things, something of a scientist and inventor. Why, for example, did the grass hidden under snow remain fresh and green?

This was not quite such a pointless question as it might seem. Bacon had been considering how best to preserve food and keep it fresh, a vital need back in the seventeenth century when fresh food was in short supply.

The snow covering the ground brought an idea into his fertile brain. He ordered his coachman to stop and buy a chicken from a smallholder at the roadside. He got the man to kill it and Sir Francis himself filled the carcass with snow. He had invented frozen chicken!

It didn't do him much good though. As a result of hanging around in the cold stuffing chickens the silly man caught a chill and he died of bronchitis at the nearby home of Lord Arundel on 9 April 1626.

It seems hard to credit it but several people have reported witnessing the phantom of a partially plucked chicken flapping around Pond Square, making loud and distressed squeaking noises before disappearing into a brick wall. It was described by witnesses as being large, white, half-plucked and running in frantic circles before disappearing. Clearly the outraged bird takes no pleasure in its pioneer role in the history of food technology!

The Frozen Chicken of Pond Square has a claim to be the most fowl of phantoms!

Holding Out His Hands For Friendship

In the 1920s, when Spiritualism was all the rage, ghost-hunters were national celebrities. They sometimes came in pairs – Mr Arthur Wyeth and Mr Walter Neal were a noted double-act.

They did not look like superstars. Mr Wyeth was a short dark plump man and Mr Neal cut a dashing military figure, belying his earlier employment as a tram driver. Both were, at this time, in their 40s. It seems that they had met in 1908 and later discovered a shared interest in psychic phenomena. Mr Neal was the one who actually saw the ghosts while Mr Wyeth possessed the ability to release them from their bounds. They were retiring and modest, it seems, but after some early successes were invited to investigate cases throughout Britain.

One such case concerned a flat in Hampstead where the occupants had been troubled by the sounding of knocking and other weird noises, such as the moving of furniture. Several members of the family had experienced vivid dreams of a strange intruder apparently dressed like a clergyman, although no-one had actually seen him while they were awake.

It was Mr Neal who first saw the apparition, apparently. He described him wandering about the flat, looking confused by furniture and people that he did not recognise. 'I could see that he was trying to make himself known to friends he thought must still be there, if only he could find them,' he said.

Mr Neal and Mr Wyeth made enquiries and found that an old man matching the description had indeed lived nearby about sixty years before. He had been very lonely, with few friends except the people who lived in this particular flat at that time and where he was always welcome.

Mr Wyeth was able to effect the release of this troubled spirit – but sadly the poor old man was still bereft and he began to search for his friends in the flat below. Another attempt to free him was made, this time successfully, and the hauntings ceased.

'There was nothing repulsive or horrifying about this poor ghost,' Mr Neal said afterwards. 'He was just a blind, lost, lonely old thing, holding out his hands for friendship and clutching the empty air.'

A mystery the ghosthunting pair might just have investigated had they been around later in the century concerned poltergeist activity in 1978 in a council flat in Beechcroft Way, off Elthorne Road at the bottom of Highgate Hill. It has been alleged that the fact that council tenants were statistically more likely to report supernatural incidents was due to the fact that the less scrupulous saw this as a way of getting a move to a more pleasant property. Not so in this case – the tenants here stressed that they had spent a lot on redecorating the flat and had no wish to leave.

However, they were being disturbed by such phenomena as heavy objects being moved by invisible means and sightings of the indistinct outline of a spectral figure. Several of their neighbours reported similar happenings.

A local clergyman performed a service of blessing and things apparently quietened down.

MEDIUM RARE

The hushed group of people huddled around the table in a darkened room waited eagerly for a word from their dear departed loved-ones. The tension was real and not a little frightening. Would the spirit guide, Tinka the Red Indian, be able to bring them the reassurance that they craved?

The séance was taking place in an unremarkable bungalow in Hampstead, home of William Roy, one of the most famous of a whole clutch of mediums who flourished around the time of the Second World War – only to be humiliatingly exposed later as a fraud!

Born in 1911 and christened William George Holroyd and a former telephone engineer, by the mid 1940s he had changed his name and become something of a celebrity. With so many bereaved by the war and longing for some communication from those they had lost, he was onto a winner. His 'clients' were charged up to £12 for a session – and attendance at each séance was restricted to no more than a dozen people.

From the start some had their suspicions about the ease with which Mr Roy, assisted by a number of his romantic spirit guides, was able to tell his clients just what they wanted to hear and how he seemed to know so much about them. Yet thousands testified to his skills and spoke of the comfort he had brought them. No less a person than Mr Mackensie King, Prime Minister of Canada, was on record as having received words from Queen Victoria and Mr Gladstone via Mr Roy's lips.

There were supposedly rigorous checks made. In 1948 the spiritualist journal *Psychic News* ran a headline: 'SPIRIT VOICES SPOKE EVEN WHEN MEDIUM'S MOUTH WAS FILLED WITH DYED WATER!' and even with his hands tied and sticking plaster put over his mouth Mr Roy was still able to transmit messages, not only in English but also, it was claimed, in Spanish, Swedish, French, Yiddish and even Malay!

But it all fell apart in 1952 when, after a row with his employer, Roy's assistant 'blew the gaffe' to the editor of *Psychic News*. He revealed to him the electrical apparatus the skilled engineer had used to produce his dramatic effects. These included a miniature loudspeaker through which the pre-recorded voices of the 'spirits' spoke to the gullible clients. Masks and swathes of butter muslin (to simulate ectoplasm) were found.

Before being admitted to the séance, the clients were asked to leave their coats in the waiting room. Once they had gone, the assistant revealed, he would go through the pockets in search of any letters, photographs or other items that would help Roy give the impression that the spirits knew things about his victims that they would not have expected to be known. It was all too easy. The assistant later withdrew his allegations but it was too late. *Psychic News* decided to press charges and Mr Roy decided to cut his losses. He undertook to leave England for South Africa.

In 1955, however, he returned and brazenly began to set up more séances and to advertise for clients once again. This was too much for Maurice Barbanell, editor of a rival journal, *Two Worlds*. He published an exposé of Roy and three similar charlatans. He then found himself being attacked with a riding crop wielded by Roy's wife, Mary Plowright, an assault for which she was later fined. Her husband started a protracted lawsuit against Barbanell but in February 1958 suddenly dropped the case.

This change of heart may have been due to his recognising that his cause was hopeless – but more likely because he had realised the financial benefits that might accrue from selling his story to the newspapers.

'Of course I am a phony,' he cheerfully admitted to the *Sunday Pictorial* as he pocketed a fat fee. 'It is true that I have tricked women at séances but I did no harm.' Indeed he was quite unrepentant: 'I know that even after this confession I could fill the séance room again with people who find it a comfort to believe that I am genuine.'

As the astronomer Patrick Moore once said about astrology, 'all it proves is that there is one born every minute!'

HUNTING THE VAMPIRE IN HIGHGATE CEMETRY

Highgate Cemetery is perhaps best known for the tomb of Karl Marx, and is still a place of pilgrimage for Communist sympathisers. The cemetery dates from 1836 when the London Cemetery Company bought seventeen acres of land on a hillside overlooking London. The site was landscaped at great expense with trees and ornamental plants, winding paths and arbours, creating an earthly paradise for the dear departed.

All this was fine so long as there were sufficient funds to maintain it and staff to do the work but gradually during the 1960s the place became overgrown and derelict. After years of neglect and vandalism the cemetery was closed to the public in 1975. There was quite an outcry and an organisation known as the Friends of Highgate Cemetery undertook the massive task of restoration and reopening.

It was during the cemetery's slow decline that stories of a resident vampire began to circulate locally. It was later alleged that a local ciné club had used the spooky location to make a horror movie and that it was their activities that brought about the trouble that followed.

On the night of Friday 13 March 1970, inspired by a television interview given by a Mr David Farrant, a 'vampire hunt' took place in the cemetery. A large crowd of people, some allegedly wearing crucifixes for protection and carrying sharpened stakes, surged through the overgrown vaults, carrying torches and determined to track down the evil presence.

They found nothing, a fact attributed by one of the prime movers, the aptly named Mr Alan Blood – a schoolteacher from Essex – to the fact that their sheer numbers and the disturbance had frightened the vampire away. People, he assured reporters, had seen 'something crawling away in the darkness'. Meanwhile Mr Farrant insisted that on several occasions he had seen 'a dark human-like shape about eight feet tall' gliding over the graves.

The maintenance staff at the cemetery were unconvinced and very angry about the £9,000 worth of damage caused to the vaults by the intruders.

Highgate cemetery.

Graves had been disturbed and on several occasions lead had been stolen from coffins and remains desecrated. Three schoolgirls were reported to have been traumatised when they came across the remains of a woman which had been dragged out of a tomb.

Mr Farrant blamed 'sinister occult groups' for these outrages. In September of the same year he was charged with 'entering enclosed premises for an unlawful purposes' having been apprehended by a policeman as he climbed over the wall of the locked cemetery at dead of night, armed with a wooden cross and a stake. He was later released and proclaimed that 'I will not rest until I catch the Vampire of Highgate Cemetery. He has to be destroyed. He is evil!' He thought that the vampire might have been unintentionally released from the vault by the activities of the ciné club.

But the legend of the cemetery vampire might have a basis in the strange tale of the remains of Lizzie Siddal, model and muse of the Pre-Raphaelite artist and poet, Dante Gabriel Rossetti. When his beloved died in 1862

Rossetti was devastated. As her open coffin lay ready for burial in Highgate Cemetery he placed manuscripts of poems that she had inspired, next to her cheek and her vibrant golden-red hair.

It was a touching romantic gesture but in time Rossetti began to regret his actions for he had lost his only copies and, now that he was becoming famous, they were valuable! He made arrangements to have Lizzie's coffin exhumed. His agent in the protracted negotiations with the Home Secretary was a Mr Howell and on a dark night in October 1869 Howell was present, along with a doctor and a solicitor, as the workmen set about their grim task by the light of lanterns and a small fire.

Rossetti himself could not bear to be present and he waited nervously for news. When Howell handed over the precious manuscript he also gave Rossetti the amazing news that Lizzie's hair remained as brightly coloured as ever and her body had not been ravaged by the passage of time.

Those who believe in vampires assert that that the dead rot while the 'undead' remain undecayed until a stake is driven through their heart. Is there some supernatural process at work here or was Howell simply trying to spare Rossetti's feelings in some way?

Peter Hough, who recounts this story in *Supernatural Britain* points out that tales of uncorrupted bodies being found in opened tombs are not uncommon. Christian saints appear over the centuries to have been particularly adept in this regard.

The Enfield Poltergeist

One of the most baffling and sinister supernatural tales of recent times is that of the Enfield Poltergeist in the late 1970s.

It all started innocently enough in August 1977 with Peggy Harper, a divorced mother of four, putting her children to bed in their three-bedroom council house. When two of the children, Janet and Pete, complained that their beds were moving, Peggy thought they were just playing silly games – especially as their beds remained perfectly still when she went up to investigate.

But the same thing happened the following night and the frightened children said that it sounded like a chair being moved across the floor. Peggy moved the chair away and thought that would be the end of it but when she switched out the light she heard the same sound. It stopped when she turned the light on, yet began again as soon as she turned it off. There were four loud knocks on the wall and a chest of drawers moved of its own volition. She moved it back against the wall but as soon as she turned her back it moved away. This sequence was repeated a second time and the now-terrified mother fled, with the children, to a neighbour's house.

The neighbours doubtless thought the whole saga was some sort of daft hoax but when they came over to the Harpers' house they heard the knocking too but could find nothing to account for it. The police were called and heard the same thing. One officer later signed a statement to the effect that he had seen a chair move across the floor of its own accord.

Things now became even more alarming. As investigations proceeded there were numerous witnesses to the paranormal happenings. A local clergyman and reporters from a national newspaper were among those who testified to seeing objects flying through the air or hearing the knockings. Maurice Grosse, a member of the Society for Psychical Research, was called in. He stayed in the house for several days, seeing and hearing nothing out of the ordinary. He must have thought that his time was being wasted but was present as a chair in one of the children's bedrooms flew across the room while the child was asleep in bed. The chair was put back but amazingly it happened an hour later, seen by a photographer who was also staying in the house. The case of the Enfield Poltergeist got wide publicity in the media and became a national obsession.

It all went on for no less than two years, during which time the embattled family endured mysterious sounds almost daily, furniture moving on its own accord, blankets pulled off beds and mysterious puddles on the floor. More than once the children claimed to have been forcibly pulled from their beds by unseen hands, claims that were backed up by their mother who said she had witnessed it happening.

Eleven-year-old Janet seemed to be at the centre of these frightening manifestations. She was seen to be thrown across the room, curtains wrapped themselves around her neck attempting to strangle her and she would often speak in a strange coarse male voice. At times she claimed to be someone called Bill. No-one in the family could have known this at the time but it was later established that a man of this name had indeed died there.

The investigators began to be suspicious. Was Janet somehow faking the whole thing? Hidden cameras caught her bending spoons with her hands and trying to bend an iron bar. The deep male voice did indeed come from her throat for hour after hour yet her normal speaking voice remained undamaged. She was taken to the specialist Maudsley Hospital in London for six weeks observation to see whether she was suffering from mental illness. The doctors decided that she was not.

Significantly, perhaps, during Janet's absence the supernatural manifestations in the house at Enfield stopped completely. One researcher, Anita Gregory, claimed that the children's uncle thought that Janet had learned the trick of talking in a deep voice and that she was a mischievious girl who delighted in playing tricks on people. Apparently, he believed that it all stemmed from Janet's personality. Certainly by now the children seemed more amused rather than frightened by the strange happenings and the national attention they got as a result. Yet after two years it all stopped suddenly and the Harper family were able to live a normal life once again.

The researcher John Zaffis, the source of a detailed report on the Enfield case that I found on the internet, seems to suggest that the children had a lot to do with it. Something unexplained may have happened at the start but, as events unfolded and they got all the publicity and attention, maybe the children let the hoax run away with them and were unable to extract themselves from a situation that was too much for them. If it was a put-up job, the investigators agree that the mother, Peggy, was unlikely to have been a party to it.

This is perhaps the most famous tale of the supernatural to come out of Middlesex. Students of the paranormal are still arguing about what really happened. Some believe it to be a 'classic' poltergeist case – others see it as an elaborate hoax.

The Crown & Horseshoes pub in Horseshoe Lane off Chase Side has a curious reputation. It is to be found tucked away from main roads in a slightly sinister and shady location a short walk from the town centre. It is approached over a narrow footbridge which crosses a straightened section of river.

In 1976 the landlord told ghost researcher Andrew Green of 'footsteps and mysterious banging of doors' in the pub, which is known to have been the scene of two sudden deaths in 1816 and 1832. Brian Bullock, a regular customer at the pub, was walking past one day and glanced in and was surprised to see an elderly woman pass one of the windows. He later asked the landlord who she was, only to be assured that the pub was completely empty at the time.

I visited the Crown & Horseshoes at the end of September 2003. The pub manager, Melanie, had taken over only three months before and had not known these stories. However, getting a dog soon afterwards brought her face to face with the fact that there was something strange about the place.

'The dog just refuses to go down into the cellar,' she told me, 'and one Sunday night after the pub had closed we were clearing up when she suddenly started barking and staring at something in the corner. I couldn't see anything there and I went into the corner and called her – but she wouldn't come over!'

The Crown and Horseshoes, Enfield.

I saw or felt nothing untoward while I was there but perhaps Melanie's dog had seen something strange and evil late on a summer's evening.

FOLLOWED AROUND

The nineteenth-century antiquarian journal, *Notes and Queries*, reported many peculiar happenings, none more strange than that recorded by a Mr T. Westwood concerning a lonely house on the edge of Enfield Chase, quoted by John H. Ingram in his book, *True Ghost Stories*. He described how he was invited to dine there by the owners, two elderly spinsters.

'I well remember my walk thither,' Mr Westwood wrote. 'It was the close of a splendid autumn afternoon. The sun had already dipped below the horizon and the front of the house projected a black shadow.'

He clearly had some sort of premonition of evil that he could not explain: 'What was there in the aspect of the pile that reminded me of a corpse? I crossed the threshold with repugnance.'

A servant led him to an upstairs room to change for dinner. As soon as he was left alone Mr Westwood became conscious of a strange shuddering sound, 'as of suppressed dread'.

Thinking it was just the sound of the wind in the chimney or a draught from the half-open door, he did not take much notice at first. But then, as he moved across the room, it seemed that the noise followed him around: 'I went to the furthest extremity of the chamber,' he wrote. 'It was there also.' By now thoroughly alarmed and unable to account for what he was experiencing, he got changed quickly and headed for the stairs, hoping to rid himself of the ominous presence.

'It was on the landing. It was on the stair. It went down with me, always the same sound of shuddering horror, faint but audible, and always close at hand. Even at the dinner table, when conversation flagged, I heard it unmistakably several times, and so near that, if there was an entity connected with it, we were two on one chair.'

Yet no-one else seemed to notice anything odd. No-one else seemed alarmed.

Mr Westwood was relieved when the dinner party broke up early as several of the other guests had long journeys home. He was very glad to be on his way: 'It was a satisfaction to breathe the fresh wholesome air of the night and feel rid at last of my shuddering incubus.' Even the dark ridge road across the top of Enfield Chase held no terrors for him.

When he met his hosts again, elsewhere, he told them what he had experienced under their roof. They smiled and said that they were so used to the sound that it had ceased to trouble them. Sometimes, they said, it would be quiet for weeks. At other times the sound would follow them all over the house – but 'it was a sound, no more, and quite harmless'.

'Perhaps so,' concluded Mr Westwood, 'but of what strange horror, not ended with this life but perpetuated in the limbo of invisible things, was that sound the exponent?'

THE SPIRIT OF THE CHASE

Ghosts are no respecters of county boundaries and one whose activities extend from Middlesex into Hertfordshire is that of Sir Geoffrey de Mandeville. He is seen as a red cloaked knight frequenting the heaths and grassland of Enfield Chase, extending to South Mimms and East Barnet. Oddly, he is alleged to work to a timetable, reappearing every six years – a cycle including 1992, 1998 and 2004.

Sir Geoffrey was Earl of Essex, one of the most powerful barons in England, holding the extensive area of land which he still apparently haunts. He was a major figure in the civil wars between King Stephen and the Empress Matilda that form the background to the Brother Cadfael novels by Ellis Peters. He played one side off against the other, exacting bribes and favours from each in turn, hence his extensive estates and his earldom.

The view of Enfield Chase from Trent Park, Cockfosters.

He died fighting in East Anglia in 1144. The contemporary chronicler Henry of Huntingdon wrote of his death: 'He made light of the wound but he died of it in a few days under excommunication. See here the just judgement of God, memorable through all ages.' In other words – it served the blighter right!

Feared and hated by many while he lived, in death Geoffrey de Mandeville became something of a cult hero. The soldiers of the Knights Templar covered his body in the distinctive habit of their Order, white with a red cross, and there was quite a tussle for the privilege of burying him. The Prior of the monastic community at Saffron Walden in Essex managed to obtain from Pope Alexander III a grant of absolution from his excommunication. By now the corpse had almost reached the status of a holy relic. Bizarrely, it was said to have been 'coffined in lead and hung in the branch of an apple tree in the Templar's preceptory in the Old Temple in London' – it must have been a very strong branch! Eventually the Templars were able to bury Sir Geoffrey under the porch by the west door in the Temple church.

Yet his spirit allegedly remains uneasy and walks his lands around Christmas. A headless hound is often the warning of his approach. He appears, dressed in armour that shines a ghostly silver in the moonlight, and wearing spurs and a red cloak.

Following in Herbert's Footsteps

Knowledgeable fans of Arsenal Football Club will not need reminding of the achievements of Herbert Chapman, the club's manager from 1925 to 1934.

What devotees will claim as the premier club of English Football – and I am not taking sides on that one – began its life in 1886 as part of the sports club of the Royal Arsenal in Woolwich and in its early days played home matches at various rented grounds in the Plumstead area. Fortunes were mixed and the location in a part of South London badly served by public transport, meant that it was difficult to build up a loyal fan base to rival those of other London clubs such as Chelsea, Tottenham Hotspur, Fulham and even what was then

Clapton Orient. In 1913 the club moved to a new ground at Highbury in North London but it was not until 1925 that the club's golden age began with the appointment of Mr Chapman.

In the years of the Chapman era the club enjoyed unparalleled success, including a first F.A. Cup triumph in 1930 and winning the Championship with record points in the 1930–31 season, going on to win it three times in the following four seasons – in 1932–3 they were only second.

No wonder Herbert Chapman became such a hero around Highbury. Such was his commitment to the club that he died in harness. Pneumonia claimed him in 1934 but he had been working in his office at the club the day before his death.

It is outside this office that Herbert's ghostly footsteps were often heard by his successors, according to Ian Cook, curator of the club's museum. Nothing was ever seen but they sensed that he was keeping a fatherly eye on them.

The offices at Arsenal's stadium were subsequently remodelled and the corridor that Herbert paced is no more. That must be confusing enough for him but how will Herbert Chapman cope in the club's new stadium at nearby Ashburnham Grove?

FLINGING HERSELF TO HER DEATH

Bruce Castle at Tottenham, now a museum, does not look like the conventional idea of a medieval fortress. What you see now is mainly eighteenth-century and very plain. There is an older core but it remains largely hidden from view. The name Bruce Castle derives from its comparatively brief association with the noble Scots family, from 1254 to 1306.

In the seventeenth century it was the home of the tragic Lady Constancia Coleraine. Imprisoned by her jealous husband in a small room above the entrance porch, she escaped and in despair flung herself from the roof on 3 November 1680. With her baby in her arms she fell onto the flagstones

Bruce Castle, Tottenham.

below and was killed instantly. It is said that each year on the anniversary of that dreadful event the castle and its grounds echo to her frenzied screams. Early in the twentieth century a local vicar held a prayer meeting in the room in an attempt to quieten the ghost.

No ghosts have actually been seen by staff working at the museum but on several occasions in recent years, according to Andrew Green, people walking past the building at night have seen what appears to be a party taking place inside. Figures of people in eighteenth century costume have been encountered close to the older parts of the building but when approached the silent revellers just melt into the walls.

Long ago when nearby Edmonton was just a country village it had a haunted house called Wire Hall. There, it was alleged, a cook had murdered a fellow servant. The resulting ghostly disturbances were so bad that the room was sealed and remained bricked up for half a century until the house was pulled down. Wire Hall had another phantom – the ghost of a farm labourer killed by a bullock.

WAILING DOGS AND A WHITE LADY

Sutton House, a red-brick Tudor mansion dating back to 1535, is a remarkable survivor to find in Homerton High Street, Hackney. When it was built, Hackney was a riverside village in the 'healthful air' of the Lea valley where Middlesex adjoined Essex. Three miles across open fields from Bishopsgate in the City of London, it was a popular retreat for the wealthy where they could be safe from the ravages of the dreaded plague. Now in the care of the National Trust, it is one of those many ancient buildings with which a number of supernatural happenings are associated.

Perhaps the strangest is that of the wailing dogs. People who have been there at night have reported hearing the sounds of dogs crying in distress when clearly no animals are in the building. They are believed to be dogs that once belonged to John Machell, a wealthy wool merchant who lived at Sutton House from 1550 to 1558. Visitors to the house can see the family coat-of-arms, which features dogs, displayed in the Little Chamber. There are, apparently, many instances of dogs being taken into the house but standing transfixed at the foot of the painted staircase, refusing to go any further.

From 1939 to 1982 Sutton House was home to the head office of a trade union, the Association of Scientific, Technical and Managerial Staffs (ASTMS). Now, trade union officers are usually hard-headed practical people, not easily influenced or disconcerted, but one worker for the Union is adamant that she saw a ghost!

Mrs Sandie Raby arrived early one morning in the reception office at the front of the building. 'No sooner had I entered the room,' she told the *Hackney Gazette* in August 1987, 'when I heard a soft rustling sound. I turned and, glancing through the glazed panel of the office door, I briefly caught sight of the figure of a lady passing by. She had shoulder-length hair and was wearing what appeared to be a white dress. In an instant the figure was gone but in that brief moment my attention was drawn to the beautiful white fan she carried in her hand.'

Mrs Raby stepped outside to ask the stranger if she could be of any assistance – and found that there was nobody there! Puzzled, she checked afterwards to see if it could have been one of her colleagues but found that she was alone in the building. When she told her story later she discovered that some of her colleagues had seen the same thing.

'I cannot say that I believed in ghosts at the time,' she told the newspaper, 'and even now I am not sure. It was something quite solid and not shadowy as one would imagine a ghost to be. But if it was not a ghost, who was the lady? Where did she come from and where did she go?'

Local rumour has it that the White Lady is Frances Machell, John's ill-starred wife, roaming the building looking for the children that she never knew in life. A memorial at St Augustine's reads, 'In this church was buried Frances, the wife of John Machell of Hackney esq. – dyed at her house in Hamerton, May 11 1574, in childbed. Deliver'd of two children, John son & heir and Frances. Buried May 21.'

Ladies come in a choice of colours at Sutton House. In the early 1990s an architect sleeping in a bedroom that is now the Exhibition Room woke to see the figure of a lady in blue hovering above his bed. On another occasion the same lady was apparently seen by a house steward who woke to find her violently shaking the bed.

For years there were rumours of a secret tunnel from Sutton House. In 1890 labourers installing a new sewerage system broke through into a portion of the tunnel and got the shock of their lives. Inside they found a skeleton of a man, clad in seventeenth-century armour, lying crumpled on the floor. He is thought to have been fleeing from Oliver Cromwell's troops as they advanced on Sutton House, trying to make his escape out onto Hackney Marshes. No-one knows where the body went after this, but a story arose that his tortured soul had returned to haunt the place where he had died.

In 1990 Sutton House was being restored by the National Trust after standing empty for several years, during which time it had been occupied by squatters and vandalised. The *Hackney Gazette* was excited by the prospect of new discoveries: 'A 500-year-old mystery over the existence of a secret tunnel in Hackney's oldest building is about to be solved,' the paper claimed, 'with plucky archaeologists ignoring a legend that it is still guarded by the ghost of a knight buried alive there.'

Speaking of the tunnel, Julie Lafferty, Secretary of the Sutton House Society said, 'it would have been a fantastic way to escape. The marshes in those days were a complete no-go area'. Mike Grey, Chair of the society was a little more cautious. 'There have been stories about a tunnel for the last hundred years,' he said, 'but no-one I have ever spoken to has been able to say where it is.'

One dedicated believer in the legend and the tunnel was Alan Heyday. On the evidence of the controversial technique of dowsing, and writing in the *Sutton House Society Journal*, he claimed that the tunnel continued under Hackney Marshes and the River Lea, beneath the railway yards at Temple

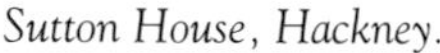

Sutton House, Hackney.

Mills and as far as the churchyard of the ancient church of St Mary's at Leyton – a distance of over three miles. He believed that it had been constructed by miners employed by Thomas Sutton, who traded in coal, earlier in the seventeenth century. To support his belief he drew attention to a group of five tower blocks in Oliver Road, Leyton. Two of the blocks are separated by a wider gap than are the others. This, the ingenious Mr Heyday stated, was because the tunnel passed between them.

Sadly for lovers of such romantic legends, when the archaeologists from the Museum of London carried out their work at Sutton House they found no evidence of the tunnel and no trace of a Civil War soldier.

There is a curious postscript to this tale of a tunnel. Its destination, St Mary's, Leyton, has its own ghosts. Leyton, just over the old boundary of Essex and now part of Greater London, was, like Hackney, a rural village until the nineteenth-century. A young man in Elizabethan clothes has been seen to glide

St Mary's church, Leyton.

through the pews of the church and disappear into a wall, upsetting nervous members of the congregation and reducing the attendance at evening services.

The Reverend R. Bren, a former vicar of Leyton, told ghosthunter Elliott O'Donnell of a curious incident in 1934: 'I entered the church one night by the south door to switch on the lights,' he recalled. 'The main switch was at that time situated at the far end of the church and I had to grope my way towards it, aided only by the feeble light given out by two dim lights under the west gallery. On turning towards the front pew I noticed two women, dressed in grey, kneeling as though in prayer. I took no notice at first then I realised that they could not have followed me into the church and certainly could not have been in the church before me. When I looked a moment later they had vanished.'

A wartime curate at the church, Reverend J.M. James (who later became vicar of St Mary's, Sunbury-on-Thames) wrote to me that 'St Mary's, Leyton, was certainly a very creepy church to enter after dark, and I well recall fumbling for the light switches that Mr Bren referred to. During the Blitz, of course, all was blacked out; but later the mercury lamps cast eerie shadows of waving branches across the windows; the old pews creaked and cracked without warning; and in the 'pea-souper' fogs of those days weird effects could be produced.'

Some might like to believe that the assorted phantoms at Leyton parish church made their escape from Sutton House and under the River Lea using the secret tunnel. But why would ghosts need a tunnel?

Bibliography

Bennett Sir Ernest *Apparitions and Haunted Homes* (Faber & Faber, 1939)

Betjeman Sir John *Metroland* (BBC TV, 1973) published in John Guest (ed.) *The Best of Betjeman* (John Murray/Penguin, 1978)

Bord Janet and Colin *Modern Mysteries of Britain* (Guild Publishing, 1987)

Bowlt Eileen M. *Ickenham and Harefield Past* (Historical Publications, 1996)

Briggs Katharine M. *A Dictionary of English Folk Tales* (Routledge & Kegan Paul, 1971)

Brooks J.A. *Ghosts of London* (Jarrold, 1982)

Carrington Hereward and Fodor Nandor *The Story of the Poltergeist* (Rider & Co., 1953)

Clegg Gillian *Chiswick Past* (Historical Publications, 1995)

Duffy Patsy 'Orbs of light going bump in the night' *Surrey Herald*, 20 August 2003

Freeman George *A History of Sunbury on Thames* (Sunbury UDC, 1974)

Gordon Stuart *The Book of Hoaxes* (Headline, 1995)

Grey Mike *Sutton House* (The National Trust, 1997)

Griffiths Zoe 'Hampton Court 'ghost' on film' (*Daily Telegraph*, 20 December 2003)

Hammond Carolyn and Peter *Chiswick in Old Photographs* (Chalford Publishing, 1994)

Herbert W.B. *Railway Ghosts and Phantoms* (David & Charles, 1989)

Hough Peter *Supernatural Britain* (Piatkus, 1995)

Ingram John H. *True Ghost Stories* (Paragon/Siena, 1998)

Jerrold Walter *Highways and Byways of Middlesex* (Macmillan, 1909)

Jones Richard *Walking Haunted London* (New Holland, 1999)

Keene C.H. 'Northolt's Ghosts' *Middlesex Quarterly* Spring 1956

King Peter 'The Laleham I knew and loved', in O.R. Adamson (ed.) *Our Dear Laleham* (Laleham Society/Ian Allan, 1989)

Larsen Egon *The Deceivers* (John Baker, 1966)

Law Ernest *A Short History of Hampton Court* (G. Bell & Sons, 1929)
Ludlam Harry (ed.) *True Stories from the Great Ghost Hunter Elliott O'Donnell* (Foulsham, 1991)
Maple Eric *Supernatural England* (Hale, 1977)
Maxwell Gordon S. *Highwayman's Heath* (Thomason, 1935; Hounslow Leisure Services, 1994)
Mee Arthur *The King's England – Middlesex* (Hodder & Stoughton, 1940)
Middlesex Federation of Women's Institutes *The Middlesex Village Book* (Countryside Books / MFWI, 1989)
Playfair Guy Lyon *This House Is Haunted* (Souvenir Press, 1980)
Robinson Nora I.A. 'Ghosts on the Move' *Middlesex Quarterly* Winter 1956
Spelthorne Local History Group *The Spelthorne Book* (Spelthorne Adult Education Institute, 1987)
Spencer John and Anne *The Encyclopaedia of Ghosts and Spirits* (Headline, 2001)
Spencer John and Anne *The Ghost Handbook* (Macmillan 1998)
Spencer John and Anne *The Poltergeist Phenomenon* (Headline, 1996)
Summers A. Leonard 'The Ghosts of Middlesex' *Middlesex Quarterly* Winter 1955
Sutherland Jonathan *Ghosts of London* (Breedon Books, 2002)
Wittich John *Discovering London Villages* (Shire Books, 1976)

There are many internet sites devoted to ghosts and the paranormal. Those which have been consulted include:
http://www.controversial.com/ghost.htm
http://guardiantales.freewebspace.com/C-Enfield.html
http://members.aol.com/MercStG2/GOSEENGPage2.html
http://www.mystical-www.co.uk/ghost/zsee.htm
http://www.unexplained-mysteries.com/articleenfield.shtml

Researchers who have posted articles on these sites include Andrew Green, George Knowles, Tony Ellis and John Zaffis.

Also – *Surrey Herald, Staines & Ashford News, Middlesex Chronicle, Middlesex Quarterly, Hackney Gazette*

• Index •